REFUTING
EVOLUTION
2

REFUTING EVOLUTION 2

JONATHAN SARFATI, Ph.D. with Mike Matthews

Master
Books

First printing: October 2002
Fourth printing: April 2005

ISBN: 0-89051-387-2
Library of Congress Number: 2002113698

Printed in the United States of America

Please visit our website for other great titles:
www.masterbooks.net

For information regarding author interviews, please contact the publicity department at (870) 438-5288.

TABLE OF CONTENTS

INTRODUCTION 7

UNIT 1: CLAIM — EVOLUTION IS SCIENCE

CHAPTER 1:   ARGUMENT: CREATIONISM IS RELIGION,
NOT SCIENCE 17

CHAPTER 2:   ARGUMENT: EVOLUTION IS COMPATIBLE WITH
CHRISTIAN RELIGION 35

CHAPTER 3:   ARGUMENT: EVOLUTION IS *TRUE* SCIENCE,
NOT "JUST A THEORY" 51

UNIT 2: CLAIM — EVOLUTION IS WELL SUPPORTED BY THE EVIDENCE

CHAPTER 4:   ARGUMENT: NATURAL SELECTION LEADS
TO SPECIATION 75

CHAPTER 5:   ARGUMENT: SOME MUTATIONS
ARE BENEFICIAL..................................... 101

CHAPTER 6:   ARGUMENT: COMMON DESIGN POINTS
TO COMMON ANCESTRY 109

CHAPTER 7:   ARGUMENT: "BAD DESIGN" IS EVIDENCE
OF LEFTOVERS FROM EVOLUTION 117

CHAPTER 8:   ARGUMENT: THE FOSSIL RECORD
SUPPORTS EVOLUTION 127

UNIT 3: CLAIM — "PROBLEMS" WITH EVOLUTION ARE ILLUSORY

CHAPTER 9:   ARGUMENT: PROBABILITY OF EVOLUTION 151

CHAPTER 10: ARGUMENT: "IRREDUCIBLE COMPLEXITY" 161

CHAPTER 11: ARGUMENT: EVOLUTION OF SEX 173

CHAPTER 12   ARGUMENT: EVOLUTION OF MANKIND 185

APPENDIX 1: COMMON ARGUMENTS FOR EVOLUTION
                       THAT HAVE BEEN REJECTED 199

APPENDIX 2: COMMON ARGUMENTS FOR CREATION
                       THAT SHOULD NOT BE USED 210

INTRODUCTION

Belief in creation is "nonsense." Creation is "a religious view that has nothing to do with science." Daily, the airwaves and newspaper racks are filled with such inflammatory claims.

The barrage of new arguments and scientific "evidence" that "prove" evolution can seem overwhelming to believers in the Word of God, who are ridiculed as irrational religious zealots who still live in the dark ages and believe the Bible's "fables" about creation. It is more crucial than ever that believers are "ready" to defend their faith (1 Pet. 3:15).

This book pulls together the most powerful arguments that Christians are likely to hear from today's leading evolutionary scientists. These arguments come from two powerhouses in the media — PBS-TV and the journal *Scientific American* — which have taken up the mantle of the pro-evolution crusade, preaching their message to a broad market around the world. PBS summarized the modern arguments for evolution in its lavish eight-hour series *Evolution,* which still airs and is shown in schools across America. It has also aired in Australia. *Scientific American* pulled together its own best arguments in a combative cover story, "15 Answers to Creationist Nonsense."

PBS TV'S *EVOLUTION* SERIES — MULTIMILLION-DOLLAR PROPAGANDA

The Public Broadcasting Service (PBS) first aired its ambitious TV series "Evolution" in September 2001. Co-produced by Clear Blue Sky Productions (founded and chaired by Microsoft billionaire Paul Allen), "Evolution" had almost unlimited funding. In addition to the TV series, the producers launched an aggressive campaign to fully equip teachers to indoctrinate young people in molecules-to-man evolution. This propaganda effort included "an unprecedented array of resources for further learning at home and in school" (their own words), including a free teacher's guide, an interactive website, a multimedia web library, teacher videos, monthly news-letters, student lessons, and teacher training workshops.

The final segment in the series, titled "What about God?" featured Answers in Genesis (AiG), a Christian ministry that shows how the scientific evidence makes sense when interpreted within the biblical world view. Ken Ham, president of Answers in Genesis, was inter-viewed for over two hours for this episode and was filmed at a live AiG seminar. The producers assured AiG that the series would be "balanced," but that proved to be untrue (as expected). Far from being "balanced," the program failed to show *any* of the scientific evidence against evolution. The real intent of the series was to show, once and for all, that evolution is true.

To avoid the impression that "Evolution" was one-sided propaganda, the producers claimed that they in-vited the Discovery Institute, part of the "intelligent design" movement,[1] for "balance." But the Discovery Institute declined because they would have been slotted

---

1. See Carl Wieland, AiG's views on the intelligent design movement, <www.answersingenesis.org/IDM>, August 30, 2002.

in the "religious" objections segments, whereas their objections to evolution are purely scientific. By failing to provide space to the scientific criticism of evolution, the PBS/Nova series gave the impression that the only criticisms of evolution are "religious." They also ignored the self-declared atheistic faith of many of evolution's proponents, including several of those involved in the series, e.g., Richard Dawkins, Daniel Dennett, the late Stephen Jay Gould, Edward O. Wilson, and Eugenie Scott.

The PBS "overview" of this program leaves no doubts about the producers' worshipful attitude toward evolution:

> Evolution plays a critical role in our daily lives, yet it is one of the most overlooked principles of life. It is the mechanism that determines who lives, who dies, and who gets the opportunity to pass traits on to the next generation, and the next, and the next. . . . Evolution [is] the underpinning of all of biology, affecting our health, our food supply and the vast web of life. . . . It's such a simple theory, yet we see millions of examples of it at work in our everyday lives. . . .
>
> The goal of "Evolution" is to heighten public awareness about what evolution is and how it works, and to dispel common misunderstandings. The project seeks to illuminate why evolution is relevant, to improve its teaching, and to encourage a national dialogue on the issues currently surrounding this science.[2]

Such in-your-face propaganda demands an answer from Christians who believe the biblical account of origins.

---

2. Evolution project overview, PBS website <http://www.pbs.org/wgbh/evolution/about/overview_project.html>.

SCIENTIFIC AMERICAN'S "15 ANSWERS TO CREATIONIST NONSENSE"

Scientific American is a semi-popular journal which publishes attractively illustrated and fairly detailed, but not overly technical, articles, mostly on science. It is not a peer-reviewed journal like *Nature* or the in-depth journal of creation, *TJ*,[3] but many of its articles are very useful.

Yet behind the surface is a deeper agenda. The most recent editors, as will be explained in this book, have been working to push an atheistic world view in the guise of "science"; and a number of corollaries, such as a radical pro-abortion, human cloning, and population control agenda.

Evidence of *Scientific American*'s agenda was its refusal to hire a science writer named Forrest Mims III after he admitted he was a creationist and pro-life. The editor who rejected Mims admitted that his work was "fabulous," "great," and "first rate," and "should be published somewhere."[4] *Scientific American* subsequently published an article about his revolutionary atmospheric haze detector, although it did not mention the incident of blatant discrimination.[5]

The current editor since late 1994, John Rennie, has fervently promoted the anti-God evolution agenda. Like many anti-creationist propagandists, he often launches into attacks with a poor understanding, and he has only a bachelor's degree in science, so is far less

---

3. Published by Answers in Genesis.
4. "Science's Litmus Test" (telephone transcript of conversation between Forrest Mims and Jonathan Piel, then editor of *Scientific American*), *Harper's Magazine* (March 1991). The transcript makes it clear that an outstanding writer was not hired for disbelieving in the sacred cow of evolution (and a "woman's right to choose" [to kill her unborn]).
5. Shawn Carlson, "The Amateur Scientist," *Scientific American* 276(5):80–81 (May 1997).

qualified than the leading creationist scientists. At the height of the controversy in Kansas over changes to de-emphasize evolution in the state education standards, Rennie personally urged scientists on university admissions committees to adopt "big stick" tactics in notifying the Kansas governor and the state board of education that "in light of the newly lowered education standards in Kansas, the qualifications of any students applying from that state in the future will have to be considered very carefully."[6] In logic, this is known as the fallacy of *Argumentum ad baculum*, i.e., "Agree with me or else unpleasant consequences will follow!" Rennie is far from the only evolutionist to resort to this.

Now Rennie has become more actively involved in the fray, taking on the role of the valiant scientist trying to stem the creationist tide. His most recent diatribe "15 Answers to Creationist Nonsense" is subtitled "Opponents of evolution want to make a place for creationism by tearing down real science, but their arguments don't hold up." Even the magazine's cover had splashed on the top, "15 ways to expose creationist nonsense."

But as will be shown, Rennie and the anti-creationist leaders that he represents have only the vaguest ideas about real creationist arguments. Many of the "creationist arguments" that they attack are "straw-man" arguments, which serious creationists have also rejected. (These bad arguments are listed in the appendix of this book.) But Rennie's other arguments in defense of evolution are also nothing new, and have been mostly answered on the Answers in Genesis website <www.AnswersInGenesis.org>. One purpose of this book is to help Christians recognize and answer the

---

6. Cited in: P. Johnson, *The Wedge of Truth: Splitting the Foundations of Naturalism* (Westmont, IL: InterVarsity Press, 2000), p. 80.

logical fallacies common among evolutionists, including inconsistent definitions of the word "evolution" — *equivocation*, and failure to differentiate between "origins science" and "operational science" (explained in detail in chapter 1). It will also point out that evolutionary belief is largely a deduction from materialistic axioms, which Rennie actually acknowledges, and lamely tries to defend.

The current *Scientific American* editor argues that creation has no place in science and has done nothing for the advancement of science. Yet he completely misses the irony that *Scientific American* was founded by a staunch believer in creation — the artist and inventor Rufus Porter (1792–1884), who thought that science glorified the Creator God. In the very first issue, his editorial stated:

> We shall advocate the pure Christian religion, without favouring any particular sect. . . .[7]

The founder of *Scientific American* also wrote an astonishing article in that issue, "Rational Religion," which bluntly declares that we all depend on the Creator God, who revealed himself in Holy Scripture. Porter's godly admonition is worth rereading:

> First, then, let us, as rational creatures, be ever ready to acknowledge God as our Creator and daily Preserver; and that we are each of us individually dependant on his special care and good will towards us, in supporting the wonderful action of nature which constitutes our existence; and in preserving us from the casualties, to which our complicated and delicate structure is liable.

7. R. Porter, "To the American public," *Scientific American* 1(1): 1845.

Let us also, knowing our entire dependence on Divine Benevolence, as rational creatures, do ourselves the honor to express personally and frequently, our thanks to Him for His goodness; and to present our petitions to Him for the favours which we constantly require. This course is rational, even without the aid of revelation: but being specially invited to this course, by the divine word, and assured of the readiness of our Creator to answer our prayers and recognize our thanks, it is truly surprising that any rational being, who has ever read the inspired writings should willingly forego this privilege, or should be ashamed to be seen engaged in this rational employment, or to have it known that he practices it.[8]

Christianity *is rational.* The purpose behind this book is to encourage believers in the absolute authority of God's revealed Word and to give them ammunition to enter the fight for the foundational truths found in Genesis, against unbelieving scientists who have been blinded by their irrational refusal to acknowledge the God who created them.

My previous book, *Refuting Evolution* (1999), gave teachers, students, and parents answers to the influential publication *Teaching About Evolution and the Nature of Science* (1998), a standard reference for science teachers produced by the U.S. National Academy of Sciences. This new book, *Refuting Evolution 2,* was inspired by two more recent statements of evolutionary beliefs: the PBS-TV series "Evolution" and the *Scientific American* broadside titled "15 Answers to Creationist Nonsense." If Christians can digest these arguments, along with the

---

8. R. Porter, "Rational Religion," *Scientific American* 1(1): 1845.

straightforward rebuttals, they will be fully equipped to answer even the best arguments thrown at them by their peers, teachers, neighbors, and nonbelievers with whom they share the gospel.

Note about citations: Quotations from the *Scientific American* article by John Rennie will be labeled *"SA,"* followed by the page number. Quotations from, and other mentions of, the PBS-TV series "Evolution," will be labeled "PBS," followed by the episode number, e.g., "PBS 6" refers to Episode 6. The seven PBS episodes have these titles:

> Episode 1: Darwin's Dangerous Idea
> Episode 2: Great Transformations
> Episode 3: Extinction!
> Episode 4: The Evolutionary Arms Race!
> Episode 5: Why Sex?
> Episode 6: The Mind's Big Bang
> Episode 7: What about God?

Creation is the Answers in Genesis international quarterly magazine. *TJ*, formerly *Creation Ex Nihilo Technical Journal*, is the Answers in Genesis international peer-reviewed journal for advanced topics in creation. In this book, it will always be cited as *"TJ."*

1

CLAIM:
EVOLUTION IS SCIENCE

Evolutionists insist that evolutionary theory
is science, and claim that creationism is religion.

CHAPTER 1

ARGUMENT: CREATIONISM IS RELIGION, NOT SCIENCE

Evolutionists say, "Creationism is a belief system
that has nothing to do with science."

The two-hour premier episode of the PBS/Nova series "Evolution" sets the tone for this propaganda effort — ridiculing biblical religion as the enemy of true science, which had long shackled scientific study. Much of the first episode is a dramatization of the life of Charles Darwin (1809–1882). It opens with Darwin's famous voyage on HMS *Beagle*. Darwin introduces himself and Captain Robert FitzRoy (1805–1865) in broken Spanish to villagers in South America. The villagers then lead Darwin and FitzRoy to the skull of an extinct ground sloth, and this conversation ensues:

> **Darwin:** I wonder why these creatures no longer exist.
> **FitzRoy:** Perhaps the ark was too small to allow them entry and they perished in the Flood.
> **D:** [laughs]
> **F:** What is there to laugh at?
> **D:** Nothing, nothing.
> **F:** Do you mock me or the Bible?

D: Neither.

F: What sort of clergyman will you be, Mr. Darwin?

D: Dreadful, dreadful.

Then the drama moves to a scene on the *Beagle,* where Captain FitzRoy is reading from Genesis 1, and Darwin is below deck rolling his eyes.

There we have it — the alleged struggle between science and "fundamentalist" religion. Of course, the representative of "fundamentalism," Captain FitzRoy, is made to spout a silly straw-man argument. Nowhere is there any hint that there could be any scientific objections to evolution.

But FitzRoy's argument is unbiblical — the Bible clearly states that two of *every* kind of land vertebrate animal was on the ark, and the ark had plenty of room for all the required animals.[1]

But then — not that we should be surprised — the PBS dramatization goes well beyond artistic license and actually falsifies history. Darwin's anti-Christianity hadn't fully developed by the time of the *Beagle* voyage, and he even attended church services, while FitzRoy, during that voyage, likely didn't believe in a global Flood. After all, FitzRoy himself had given Darwin a welcoming gift of the long-age–advocating book *Principles of Geology* by Charles Lyell (1797–1875), which was a great inspiration for Darwin's evolutionary ideas, as will be shown later in this book.

PHILOSOPHICAL ASSUMPTION BEHIND "MODERN SCIENCE" — NATURALISM

The media is not subtle about its ridicule of "creation science." John Rennie, editor-in-chief of *Scientific*

---

1. J. Sarfati, "How Did All the Animals Fit on Noah's Ark?" *Creation* 19(2):16–19 (March–May 1997); J. Woodmorappe, *Noah's Ark: A Feasibility Study* (El Cajon, CA: Institute for Creation Research, 1996).

American, gets right to the point in "15 Answers to Creationist Nonsense." He asserts,

> "Creation science" is a contradiction in terms. A central tenet of modern science is methodological naturalism — it seeks to explain the universe purely in terms of observed or testable natural mechanisms. [*SA* 84]

Now we get to the key issue. It's not about scientific facts at all, but self-serving materialistic "rules of the game" by which the evolutionary establishment interprets the facts. So it should be instructive for people to understand what's really driving Rennie and his ilk — a materialist or naturalist agenda that excludes God. This is not a tenet deducible by the experimental method, but a philosophical assumption from *outside* science.

Rennie illustrates his view of "modern science" with an example from physics:

> Physics describes the atomic nucleus with specific concepts governing matter and energy, and it tests those descriptions experimentally. Physicists introduce new particles, such as quarks, to flesh out their theories only when data show that the previous descriptions cannot adequately explain observed phenomena. The new particles do not have arbitrary properties, moreover — their definitions are tightly constrained, because the new particles must fit within the existing framework of physics. [*SA* 84–85]

What has this to do with evolution? Creationists agree that the particles would not behave arbitrarily, because they were created by a God of order. But an atheist has no philosophical justification from his underlying religious premise, i.e., "God does not exist," for a belief in an orderly universe.

DECEPTIVE ATTACKS ON CREATION "SCIENCE"

Evolutionists tend to lump all opponents of materialistic "science" under the same category, whether they call it "creation science" or "intelligent design," ignoring the profound differences among the various camps. As a result, they make some outlandish claims that simply do not apply to Bible-believing Christians. For instance, *Scientific American* attacks "creation science" because it promotes some shadowy intelligence that is beyond scientific inquiry and that offers few answers to scientific questions:

> Intelligent-design theorists invoke shadowy entities that conveniently have whatever unconstrained abilities are needed to solve the mystery at hand. Rather than expanding scientific inquiry, such answers shut it down. (How does one disprove the existence of omnipotent intelligences?)
>
> Intelligent design offers few answers. For instance, when and how did a designing intelligence intervene in life's history? By creating the first DNA? The first cell? The first human? Was every species designed, or just a few early ones? Proponents of intelligent-design theory frequently decline to be pinned down on these points. They do not even make real attempts to reconcile their disparate ideas about intelligent design. [*SA* 85]

In reality, the founders and leaders of modern "creation science" base their views on the Bible, believing it is God's inspired account of history given to mankind. It is wrong to confuse this group with other, more recent advocates of "intelligent design" who wish to avoid all appeals to biblical authority. Christians don't advocate just any "designer" who may or may not be capricious. Rather, they identify the Designer with the faithful triune God of the Bible.

We base our science on the biblical framework of history, which provides much information about when and how the Designer performed special acts of design. That is, during creation week about 6,000 years ago, He created distinct kinds of creatures. Shortly after that, Adam sinned and brought death and mutations into the world. About 1,500 years later, God judged the world by a global flood that produced most of the world's fossils. But two of every kind of land vertebrate (seven of the few "clean" ones and birds) were rescued on an ocean-liner–sized ark. After they landed on the mountains of Ararat, the ark animals migrated and diversified, adapting to different environments — including some speciation. Mankind disobeyed God's command to fill the earth, and migrated only when God confused the languages at Babel about 100 years later. This explains why human fossils are higher in the post-Flood fossil record than other mammals.

Evolutionists often attack advocates of intelligent design for perfectly admissible types of logical arguments (which evolutionists also use). For instance, *Scientific American* condemns advocates of intelligent design because "they pursue argument by exclusion — that is, they belittle evolutionary explanations as far-fetched or incomplete and then imply that only design-based alternatives remain." [*SA* 85]

This is not wrong. It is simple logic, called the law of the excluded middle.[2] Evolutionists from Darwin to today

2. J.D. Sarfati, "Loving God with All Your Mind: Logic and Creation," *TJ* 12(2):142–151 (1998).

have used the same tactic, i.e., "God wouldn't have done it that way, therefore evolution must explain it."

It's notable that Darwin often used pseudo-theological arguments *against* design rather than direct arguments *for* evolution. But this form of argument presupposes the "two-model approach," i.e., that creation and evolution are the only alternatives, so evidence against creation is evidence for evolution. Ironically, many evolutionists scream loudly if creationists use this same form of logic to conclude that evidence against evolution is support for creation!

Scientific American goes on to claim:

> Logically, this is misleading: even if one naturalistic explanation is flawed, it does not mean that all are. [*SA* 85]

This attack overlooks the obvious fact that the "intelligent design" arguments are based on *analogy*, a common scientific procedure, about what we can observe being produced by intelligent and unintelligent causes. There is nothing wrong or "misleading" about that approach. The article continues with another misleading objection:

> Moreover, it does not make one intelligent-design theory more reasonable than another. Listeners are essentially left to fill in the blanks for themselves, and some will undoubtedly do so by substituting their religious beliefs for scientific ideas. [*SA* 85]

Here *Scientific American* is accusing their opponents of doing something that evolutionists do all the time. Editor John Rennie has no objection to substituting (and confusing) his own atheistic religious ideas for scientific ones, but he finds it offensive when other people's religious ideas are brought into the discussion!

CONFUSING "ORIGINS SCIENCE" WITH "OPERATIONAL SCIENCE"; THE REAL ORIGINS OF SCIENCE

Scientific American also repeats the common claim that evolution and "methodological naturalism" are the basis for modern advances in science:

> Time and again, science has shown that methodological naturalism can push back ignorance, finding increasingly detailed and informative answers to mysteries that once seemed impenetrable: the nature of light, the causes of disease, how the brain works. Evolution is doing the same with the riddle of how the living world took shape. [*SA* 85]

This fails to note the distinction between *normal (operational) science*, and *origins* or *historical science*.[3] Normal (operational) science deals only with repeatable observable processes in the *present*, while origins science helps us to make educated guesses about origins in the *past*.

Operational science has indeed been very successful in understanding the world, and has led to many improvements in the quality of life, e.g., putting men on the moon and curing diseases. And it's vital to note that many historians, of a wide number of religious persuasions, from Christians to atheists, point out that the founders of operational science were motivated by their belief that the universe was made by a rational Creator. An orderly universe makes perfect sense only if it were made by an orderly Creator. But if atheism or polytheism were true,

---

3. N.L. Geisler and J.K. Anderson, *Origin Science: A Proposal for the Creation-Evolution Controversy* (Grand Rapids, MI: Baker Books, 1987).

then there is no way to deduce from these belief systems that the universe is (or should be) orderly.

Genesis 1:28 gives us permission to investigate creation, unlike say animism or pantheism that teach that the creation itself is divine. And since God is sovereign, He was free to create as He pleased. So where the Bible is silent, the only way to find out how His creation works is to *experiment*, not rely on man-made philosophies as did the ancient Greeks.

These founding scientists, like modern creationists, regarded "natural laws" as *descriptions* of the way God upholds His creation in a *regular* and *repeatable* way (Col. 1:15–17), while miracles are God's way of upholding His creation in a special way for special reasons. Because creation *finished* at the end of day 6 (Gen. 2:1–3), creationists following the Bible would expect that God has since mostly worked through "natural laws" except where He has revealed in the Bible that He used a miracle. And since "natural laws" are descriptive, they cannot prescribe what cannot happen, so they cannot rule out miracles. Scientific laws do not cause or forbid anything any more than the outline of a map causes the shape of the coastline.

Because creation *finished* at the end of day 6, biblical creationists would try to find natural laws for every aspect of operation science, and would not invoke a miracle to explain any repeating event in nature *in the present,* despite *Scientific American*'s scare tactics. This can be shown in a letter I wrote to an inquirer who believed that atoms had to be held together by miraculous means:

> "Natural laws" also help us make predictions about future events. In the case of the atom, the explanation of the electrons staying in their orbitals is the positive electric charge and large mass of the nucleus. This enables us to make predictions

about how strongly a particular electron is held by a particular atom, for example, making the science of chemistry possible. While this is certainly an example of Colossians 1:17, simply saying "God upholds the electron" doesn't help us make predictions.

And in my days as a university teaching assistant before joining AiG, I marked an examination answer *wrong* because it said "God made it so" for a question about the frequency of infrared spectral lines, instead of discussing atomic masses and force constants.

So, *Scientific American* is wrong to imply that creationists are in any way hindered in real operational scientific research, either in theory or in practice.

In contrast, evolution is a speculation about the unobservable and unrepeatable *past*. Thus, it comes under *origins science*. Rather than observation, origins science uses the principles of *causality* (everything that has a beginning has a cause[4]) and *analogy* (e.g., we observe that intelligence is needed to generate complex coded information in the present, so we can reasonably assume the same for the past). And because there was no material intelligent designer for life, it is legitimate to invoke a non-material designer for life. Creationists invoke the miraculous only for origins science, and as shown, this does *not* mean they will invoke it for operational science.

The difference between operational and origins science is important for seeing through common silly assertions such as:

> . . . evolution is as thoroughly established as the picture of the solar system due to Copernicus, Galileo, Kepler, and Newton.[5]

4. J.D. Sarfati, "If God Created the Universe, Then Who Created God?" *TJ* 12(1)20–22 (1998).
5. Levitt as quoted by L.S. Lerner in *Good Science, Bad Science: Teaching Evolution in the States* (Thomas B. Fordham Foundation, 2000).

However, we can *observe* the motion of the planets, but no one has ever observed an information-increasing change of one type of organism to another.

To explain further: the laws that govern the *operation* of a computer are not those that made the computer in the first place. Much anti-creationist propaganda is like saying that if we concede that a computer had an intelligent Designer, then we might not analyze a computer's workings in terms of natural laws of electron motion through semiconductors, and might think there are little intelligent beings pushing electrons around instead. Similarly, believing that the genetic code was originally designed does not preclude us from believing that it works entirely by the laws of chemistry involving DNA, RNA, proteins, etc. Conversely, the fact that the coding machinery works according to reproducible laws of chemistry does not prove that the laws of chemistry were sufficient to build such a system from a primordial soup. The PBS producer even admitted that the naturalistic origin of life was a major problem for evolution.

For some specifics, it's notable that *creationists* have made many of the great scientific advances that *Scientific American* and other evolutionary magazines like to mention! Isaac Newton discovered the spectrum of light (as well as co-inventing calculus and formulating the laws of motion and gravity); James Clerk Maxwell discovered the laws of electromagnetism which led to the prediction of electromagnetic radiation; Louis Pasteur formulated the germ theory of disease and disproved spontaneous generation; Joseph Lister pioneered antiseptic surgery; Raymond Damadian pioneered magnetic resonance imaging (MRI) that is a vital tool in brain research.

In spite of the evidence, *Scientific American* asserts,

Creationism, by any name, adds nothing of intellectual value to the effort. [*SA* 85]

This blind assertion shows John Rennie's willing ignorance concerning the contributions made by creationists to the major branches of modern science in general and to his own magazine in particular.

EXAMPLE OF THE NATURALISTIC ASSUMPTIONS DRIVING EVOLUTION

Scientists have a reputation for impartiality and rigid honesty in their treatment of the facts, but it does not take much digging to find examples of how powerfully a materialistic mindset can cloud a scientist's judgment. One of the greatest influences on Darwin, for example, was a book he took on the *Beagle* voyage, *Principles of Geology* by Charles Lyell, which pushed the idea of slow and gradual geological processes occurring over millions of years, and denied Noah's flood. Modern evolutionists acknowledge that Lyell was biased and unscientific, driven by anti-biblical philosophical assumptions, whereas the "catastrophists" of his day (who believed in one or more Flood catastrophes) were rigid followers of the scientific method. Stephen Jay Gould (1941–2002), himself a leading evolutionist, wrote:

Charles Lyell was a lawyer by profession, and his book is one of the most brilliant briefs published by an advocate. . . . Lyell relied upon true bits of cunning to establish his uniformitarian views as the only true geology. First, he set up a straw man to demolish. In fact, the catastrophists were much more empirically minded than Lyell. The geologic record does seem to require catastrophes:

rocks are fractured and contorted; whole faunas are wiped out. To circumvent this literal appearance, Lyell imposed his imagination upon the evidence. The geologic record, he argued, is extremely imperfect and we must interpolate into it what we can reasonably infer but cannot see. The catastrophists were the hard-nosed empiricists of their day, not the blinded theological apologists.[6]

One infamous example of Lyell's bias was his decision to ignore eyewitness accounts of the rate of erosion of Niagara Falls, and publish a different figure to suit his purpose.[7]

But Lyell convinced Darwin, who eventually linked slow and gradual geological processes with slow and gradual biological processes. For example, he said that mountains were products of thousands of small rises. PBS Episode 1 portrays Darwin saying, "Time, unimaginable tracts of time, is the key," and arguing that just as small changes over ages can throw up mountains, why couldn't small changes accumulate over ages in animals to produce new structures?

Not only Darwin, but also many prevailing churchmen of his day had capitulated to Lyell's ideas. The prominent view was that God created organisms in their present locations. In his arguments against creation and for evolution, Darwin wondered why God would create not-quite-identical finches in almost identical islands.

In this case, Darwin rightly thought that the island animals were descended from mainland ones. But this is what biblical creationists would believe too, with a global flood and subsequent migration from Ararat via

---

6. S.J. Gould, *Natural History* (February 1975): p. 16.
7. L. Pierce, "Niagara Falls and the Bible," *Creation* 22(4):8–13 (September–November 2000).

continents to islands. So Darwin's arguments work only against a compromised creationist view, not the biblical view. (Present-day "progressive creationists" hold essentially the same view as Darwin's opponents, so they are trying to fight a battle that was lost 150 years ago — but wouldn't have been if Christians had not compromised on the earth's age and the global flood.)

Darwin's attempt to explain variations between finches underscores a fundamental point in the debate between evolution and creation: that facts do not speak for themselves, but are always *interpreted* within a framework. Creationists don't deny a single *observation* an evolutionist makes, but find that they virtually always make better sense when interpreted within the biblical framework, as opposed to a compromised one. Therefore, it shouldn't be surprising that many of the alleged "evidences" for evolution actually turn out to support the biblical model.

SCOPES TRIAL AND *SPUTNIK*

Evolutionists frequently point to two emotion-charged incidents in the 20th century that supposedly confirm the danger of mixing creation and science — the famous Scopes trial (1925) and the launch of *Sputnik* (1957). PBS 7 talks about the Scopes trial and says that William Jennings Bryan was victorious, and that it had the "chilling effect" of expunging evolution from science curricula from many states. Surprisingly, for a series containing millions of dollars worth of misinformation, it didn't present the play and film *Inherit the Wind* as a serious account of the trial. A good thing, because of its gross distortions documented in the article "*Inherit the Wind* — an Historical Analysis."[8]

8. D. Menton, "*Inherit the Wind* — an Historical Analysis," *Creation* 19(1):35–38 (December 1996–February 1997); see also <www.answersingenesis.org/scopes>.

Then PBS 7 showed *Sputnik,* and claimed that American authorities were so alarmed that the Soviets beat them into space that they decided to make science education a priority. Somehow, evolution was smuggled in there. However, the science that put spacecraft on the moon is nothing like evolution. Rocket science involves repeatable experiments in the observable *present*; evolution is a just-so story to explain the unobservable *past* without God's direct intervention. It's especially ironic that the leader of the Apollo program, Wernher von Braun, was a creationist!

It's also blatantly revisionist history to claim that the Scopes trial paved the way for the *Sputnik.* During this alleged scientific nadir between Scopes and *Sputnik,* American schools produced more Nobel prizes than the rest of the world combined. America produced *twice* as many as all other countries — this was especially pronounced in the biological field (physiology and medicine), supposedly one that can't do without evolution. The Soviet Union beat the USA into space merely because the totalitarian government made it a top priority. While the USA had a good space program, there were other spending priorities, such as helping a war-torn world to rebuild. When the USA put its mind to it, it quickly surpassed the USSR, and was the first to land men on the moon in 1969. If it had needed scientists trained in evolution, the moon landing wouldn't have happened till the next generation had gone through the public school system.[9]

PBS and science journals are not the only ones trying to equate "science" with evolution. One of the most vociferous anti-creationist organizations is the pretentiously

9. The Discovery Institute's critique makes these good points in *Getting the Facts Straight: A Viewer's Guide to PBS's Evolution* (Seattle, WA: Discovery Institute Press, 2001).

named National Center for Science Education. This is a humanist-founded organization, and its chief spokesperson, Eugenie Scott, is the winner of humanist awards and was also a consultant for the PBS series. It's significant that the only "science education" NCSE seems interested in is evolution — not chemistry, physics, astronomy, or even experimental biology (or rocket science for that matter).[10]

CREATION IN PUBLIC SCHOOLS?

The debate about religion and science has practical ramifications today, and it has spilled over into the public schools again. Evolutionists are terrified that criticisms of evolution (which they equate with teaching biblical creation — when it suits them!) may be allowed into the schools, and they are doing everything they can to stop it. (It's important to note that, although it would be nice to give teachers the *freedom* to present alternatives to evolution, Answers in Genesis and other major creationist organizations have *not* been lobbying for compulsory creation in schools, despite common accusations. For one thing, one school of thought is that sending kids to public schools is like Joshua sending the Israelite children to Canaanite schools. But mainly, would Christians want an atheistic teacher to be forced to teach creation, and deliberately distort it?)

PBS 7 extensively featured Jefferson High School in Lafayette, Indiana. A student petition requested that the science curriculum should include the creation model. One teacher admitted that the signatories included "outstanding students" and even some teachers. Of course this shows that one can be a top student without swallowing the evolutionary story.

---

10. See "How Religiously Neutral Are the Anti-Creationist Organizations?" <http://www.answersingenesis.org/docs/189.asp> and "A Who's Who of Evolutionists," *Creation* 20(1):32 (December 1997–February 1998).

But several teachers claimed the petition was dangerous (i.e., for them to listen to students and parents). One teacher, Clare McKinney, claimed to be a Christian, but she claimed that science can't involve God, swallowing the belief that science and religion do not overlap. Yet this claim is only possible if the Bible and the real world have nothing to do with each other, or if God and reason are mutually exclusive.

Another teacher at the school said that science is peer-reviewed, testable, and repeatable. He failed to explain how a claim such as "a reptile turned into a bird 150 million years ago" is testable or repeatable! Although evolutionists like to condemn creation as non-science, they have a hard time coming up with a definition of "science" that includes evolution and excludes creation unless it's blatantly self-serving. Sometimes these definitions are self-contradictory, e.g., some evolutionists, including Gould, have claimed that creation is not scientific because it's not *testable*, then explained how it has allegedly been *tested* and shown to be wrong.

The school board, led by School Superintendent Ed Eiler, refused the Jefferson High School petition, claiming that creation is not part of science. Amazingly, the teacher Clare McKinney lamented how biology would be unteachable if evolution were censored, but that was *not* what the petitioners requested. Ironically, they wanted the curriculum to teach *more* about evolution than the establishment wants the students to learn! But the upshot was that any criticisms of evolution are censored instead.

There are numerous instances of teachers who face severe discrimination simply because they want to present their classes with the *scientific* evidence against evolution. One chemistry teacher was constructively dismissed simply for having Answers in Genesis speaker Geoff Stevens address his class on chemical evolution, surely an appropriate topic for chemistry class. Mr. Stevens presented a purely scientific case that non-living chemicals could not form a living cell by natural processes (see chapter 9), and he didn't mention God or religion at all. But Eiler issued a formal letter of reprimand to the teacher of the class, Dan Clark, falsely accusing him of introducing "religion" to his classes. The real problem was that ardent evolutionists refused to tolerate any challenges to their materialist faith.[11]

When tested by logic and reality, the evolutionists' contention that "creationism is a religion that has nothing to do with science" is hypocritical. Both creationists and evolutionists accept the same facts of science, they just interpret them based on different frameworks. One interpretation is based on atheistic materialism, and the other is based on God's perfect, revealed Word.

11. S. Byers, "Chemistry Teacher Resigns Amid Persecution,"
 <http://www.answersingenesis.org/docs2001/0918news.asp>.

CHAPTER 2

ARGUMENT: EVOLUTION IS COMPATIBLE WITH CHRISTIAN RELIGION

Evolutionists say, "Evolution is not necessarily antithetical to Christianity—science and religion just deal with different realms of knowledge."

Though the media love to attack *creation* as unscientific, they're too canny to appear blatantly anti-*Christian*. In fact, they typically downplay the rabidly atheistic faith of many leading evolutionists. The PBS series "Evolution," for example, invited several virulent atheists, such as Stephen Jay Gould and Eugenie Scott,[1] to speak on their program; but it breathed not a word about their strongly held religious views and open assaults on Christianity. Such outspoken atheism does not play well in religious America.

IS DARWINISM ANTI-CHRISTIAN?

The opening episode of the *Evolution* series is aptly titled "Darwin's Dangerous Idea," presumably inspired

---

1. D. Batten, "A Who's Who of Evolutionists," *Creation* 20(1):32 (December 1997 – February 1998).

by Daniel Dennett's book of the same name. Dennett argues that Darwin should be ranked ahead of Newton and Einstein as a scientific genius, because he united the disparate world of purposelessness and meaninglessness with the world of purpose and meaning. "Evolution's" producers acknowledge that Darwin's idea posed a "threat" to the established views of his day, but they omit Dennett's famous insight that Darwinism was "universal acid," eating through every traditional idea, especially "meaning coming from on high and being ordained from the top down." Presumably that would have alerted the Christian viewers too soon.

Annie's death and the problem of evil

PBS 1 dramatizes a turning point in the spiritual life of Charles Darwin — the sickness and death of his beloved daughter, Annie. Although the series does not spell it out, Darwin's biographer James Moore makes it clear that this tragedy destroyed the truth of Christianity in Darwin's mind. How could there be a good God if He allowed this to happen? Instead, Darwin decided that Annie was an unfortunate victim of the laws of nature, i.e., she lost the struggle for existence.

Annie's death raised serious questions about God's goodness, but the prevailing view of Darwin's day — that the earth was old and had long been filled with death and violence — provided no adequate answers. Alas, the church adopted this prevailing view, which placed fossils millions of years *before* Adam. This view entails that death and suffering were around for millions of years before Adam, and yet God called His acts of creation "very good." Such a view evidently didn't appeal to Darwin. It's sad that many church leaders today still promote theistic evolution (the belief that God divinely ordained evolution — the struggle for survival and death — as His method of creation) and progressive creation (the belief that the "days" of creation in Genesis 1 refer to long ages of death and suffering). Both of these compromise views[2] have the insuperable problem of allowing death before sin. However, the proponents of these views claim that they are *more* acceptable to unbelievers than the literal Genesis view, failing to realize that this battle was already lost in Darwin's day.

Yet the Bible is very clear the earth has a "young" age (i.e., about 6,000 years), and the events described in Genesis 1–3 perfectly explain how God could be good and yet the earth be filled with death and suffering. The Bible says that God created everything "very good" (Gen. 1:31), whereas death is an intruder, called "the last enemy" (1 Cor. 15:26). God did *not* introduce death and suffering millions of years ago — as many church leaders were saying in Darwin's time — instead, suffering was the direct result of Adam's sin (Gen. 2:17, 3:19; Rom. 5:12–19, 8:20–22; 1 Cor. 15:21–22). To any Bible believer, this truth entails that the fossil record — a record of death, disease, and suffering — must date *after* Adam's sin.

In the end, Darwin concluded that Christianity is a "damnable doctrine" because his unbelieving father would be condemned to hell, but of course the PBS episode doesn't mention this! It does, however, show Darwin's older brother Erasmus (named after their evolutionary grandfather) mocking hymn singing in church.

Kenneth Miller — a good Christian and an evolutionist?

While PBS 1 attempted to mute Darwin's obvious anti-Christianity, it prominently featured Kenneth Miller, who claims to be "an orthodox Catholic and an

---

2. See <www.answersingenesis.org/compromise> for more information.

orthodox Darwinist." He wrote a book, *Finding Darwin's God*, an anti-creationist polemic, to try to reconcile God and evolution. Miller has had a long history of joining forces with leading humanists against creation, and his book is full of straw-man arguments, misinformation, and outright deception.[3] The last sentences in his book are revealing: "What kind of God do I believe in? . . . I believe in Darwin's God."[4] Since Darwin was anti-Christian, as shown above, this is not the God any Christian can believe in. But PBS 1 shows Miller attending mass and taking communion, hoping that this show of outward religiosity will convince people who prefer outward appearances to inward convictions (cf. Matt. 23:25–28).

Religion and science — "non-overlapping magisteria"?

Despite Darwin's obvious anti-Christianity, evolutionists like to say that Darwin didn't intend to disparage ideas of God. In fact, PBS 1 quotes evolutionist Stephen Jay Gould saying so. This is consistent with Gould's widely publicized claims that religion and science are "non-overlapping magisteria" (NOMA).[5] That is, science deals with facts of the real world, while religion deals with ethics, values, morals, and what it means to be human.

However, this is based on the philosophically fallacious "fact-value distinction," and is really an anti-Christian claim. For example, the resurrection of Christ is an essential "value" of the Christian faith (1 Cor. 15:12–19),

3. For a thorough refutation of Miller's book, see J. Woodmorappe and J. Sarfati, "Mutilating Miller," *TJ* 15(3): 29–35, 2001.
4. Kenneth R. Miller, *Finding Darwin's God* (New York, NY: Cliff Street Books, 1999).
5. S.J. Gould, *Rocks of Ages: Science and Religion in the Fullness of Life* (New York, NY: Ballantine, 1999).

but it must also be a *fact* of history to be of value — it had to pass the "testable" Bible prophecy that the tomb would be empty on the third day; and it had to impinge on science by demonstrating the power of God over so-called "natural laws" that dead bodies decay, and do not return to life. Christians should be aware that this is not only a theoretical argument about the anti-Christian implications of NOMA — Gould openly dismissed John's *historical* narrative of Jesus' post-resurrection appearance to doubting Thomas as a "moral tale."[6]

This NOMA distinction really teaches that religion is just in one's head, which seems to dull the senses of many Christians more than an overt declaration that Christianity is false. So NOMA is even more insidious.

Christians should not fall for this false distinction between facts and morality. Christ is the Lord of the universe, and the Bible is accurate on everything it touches on, not just faith and morality, but history, science, and geography, also. So Christians should not give up any part of the "real world" to those with a materialistic agenda — especially when atheists are happy to let their own faith influence their science, by promoting evolution.

Gould's real anti-Christian sentiments are shown by his 1990 lecture at Victoria University of Wellington, New Zealand. The whole theme of his lecture was that Darwin deliberately tried to counter the argument from design, and Gould speculated that this was because FitzRoy had browbeaten him with this argument. Gould also addressed the popular notion that evolution can be reconciled with religion and purpose because evolution is supposedly "progress." Gould slammed this idea, saying that

---

6. Gould, *Rocks of Ages*, p. 14.

evolution was just a blind, purposeless struggle for existence.[7] It seems that science and "God" are compatible only when trying to pacify concerned Christians, but at other times Gould makes it clear that there's no room for God, at least in the "real world."

None other than Kenneth Miller, who was impressed by Gould's NOMA idea, when he saw documentation of Gould's true feelings about belief in God, conceded that creationists had a point when they accused Gould of double talk:

> Some wonder if Gould, in his heart, really believes these words. Late in 1997, Phillip Johnson described Gould's essay as "a tissue of half-truths aimed at putting the religious people to sleep, or luring them into a 'dialogue' on terms set by the materialists." Had Johnson seen Gould on television a year later, his sense of Gould's duplicity might have been dramatically confirmed:
>
> INTERVIEWER: Gould disputes the religious claim that man is at the center of the universe. The idea of a science-religious dialogue, he says, is "sweet" but unhelpful.
>
> [Speaking to Gould]: Why is it sweet?
>
> GOULD: Because it gives comfort to many people. I think that notion that we are all in the bosom of Abraham or are in God's embracing love is — look, it's a tough life and if you can delude yourself into thinking that there's all some warm and fuzzy meaning to it all, it's enormously comforting. But I do think it's just a story we tell ourselves.

7. For an accurate account of Gould's lecture, see C. Wieland, "Darwin's Real Message: Have You Missed It?" *Creation* 14(4):16–19 (September–November 1992).

Hard to see how something Gould regards as "just a story we tell ourselves" could also be an obligatory step in "the attainment of wisdom."[8]

On PBS 1, Stephen Jay Gould said that Darwinism answers who we are, as far as science can answer that question. Boston University biologist Chris Schneider said that evolution "stirs the soul." The episode ends with a comment by Darwin's biographer, James Moore: "Darwin's vision of nature was, I believe, fundamentally a religious vision." In the light of this, it's amazing that the series persists in claiming that evolution is "science" rather than "religion."

Deep time — the truth seeps out

Despite cunning efforts to deceive people that evolution and Christianity are compatible, the truth eventually leaks out. Probably everyone has seen one of the cute illustrations that show man's tiny place on the "yardstick of time." In PBS 2, for example, Neil Shubin, a paleontologist from the University of Chicago, shares his version of the story. He claims that the earth is 4.5 billion years old; and to show how insignificant humans are, he scales this time to one hour. Then he claims that animals existed only in the last 10 minutes, while humans appeared only in the last 100th of a second.

Despite the PBS series' claim to be respectful of Christianity, this is one of many examples of the direct contradiction between evolution/billions of years and Christ's teachings. Jesus says in Mark 10:6, "But *from the beginning of the creation*, God made them male and female." This statement is consistent with Christ's belief in a literal interpretation of Genesis, which teaches that the earth was created about 4,000 years before He spoke

---

8. Miller, *Finding Darwin's God.*

those words. Adam and Eve were created on day 6, which on the scale of 4,000 years is almost indistinguishable from the beginning. But this time frame is diametrically opposed to Shubin's illustration, which has man appearing almost at the end, not the beginning."[9]

WHAT ABOUT GOD?

"What about God?" is the title of the final episode (7) in the PBS series, "Evolution." To the very end, the producers tried to obscure the obvious — that evolution and biblical Christianity are diametrically opposed. Actually, they hardly discussed *biblical* Christianity, but interviewed people who believe that "God" used evolution. As is typical of most evolutionists, they acknowledge biblical Christianity and even interview representatives of it, but they omit the strongest case of the best defenders, and give much airtime to those who haven't the faintest idea about defending biblical Christianity. But the PBS program was honest about one thing: it clearly showed examples of the baneful effects of compromise among Christians, and these incidents should raise alarms among pastors that they have an obligation to exhort their flock to be ready with answers, as the apostle Peter commanded in 1 Peter 3:15.

Concealing the truth about "fundamentalist" concerns

The PBS narrator (Liam Neeson) talks about the views of "Christian fundamentalists like Ken Ham" (president of Answers in Genesis Ministries in the United States), but he never defines the word, of course. Presumably, the producers hope to exploit modern connotations of the

---

9. There are also many scientific problems with any assertions that the earth looks old. The conflicts between billions of years with the words of Christ and true science are well outlined in C. Wieland, "The Earth: How Old Does it Look?" *Creation* 23(1):8–13 (December 2000–February 2001).

word, and their attempt at name-calling received an un-
expected bonus after the 2001 terrorist attack against the
United States, attributed to Muslim "fundamentalists."
But this modern usage of the term reflects ignorance of
its original honorable meaning:

> Historically, fundamentalism has been used
> to identify one holding to the five fundamentals
> of the faith adopted by the General Assembly of
> the Presbyterian Church of the USA in 1910. The
> five fundamentals were the miracles of Christ, the
> virgin birth of Christ, the substitutionary atone-
> ment of Christ, the bodily resurrection of Christ,
> and the inspiration of Scripture.[10]

Of course, Mr. Ham and AiG as a whole uncompro-
misingly affirm fundamentalism in its historic sense.

The PBS narrator scornfully dismisses Mr. Ham as
one of those who teach a literal interpretation of the
creation account in Genesis. This is a common tactic
among evolutionists, who imply that there is something
unusual about taking Genesis literally, but they completely ignore what "fundamentalists" teach about interpreting historical narrative as historical narrative,
interpreting poetry as poetry, and making distinctions
between them.[11]

The Hebrew grammar of Genesis shows that Genesis 1–11 has the same literary style as Genesis 12–50,
which no one doubts is historical narrative. For example,
the early chapters of Genesis frequently use the construc-
tion called the "*waw* consecutive," usually an indicator
of historical sequence. Genesis 1–11 also has several other
trademarks of historical narrative, such as "accusative

---

10. P. Enns, *Moody Handbook of Theology* (Chicago, IL: Moody Press, 1989), p. 613.
11. See R. Grigg, "Should Genesis Be Taken Literally?" *Creation* 16(1):38–41
(December 1933–February 1994).

particles" that mark the objects of verbs, and terms that are often carefully defined. And the Hebrew verb grammar of Genesis 1 has a particular feature that fits *exactly* what would be expected if it were representing a series of past events. That is, only the first verb is perfect, while the verbs that continue the narrative are imperfect. In Genesis 1, the first verb is *bara* (create) which is perfect, while the subsequent verbs that move the narrative forward are imperfect. But parallelisms, which are characteristic of Hebrew poetry, are absent from Genesis, except where people are cited, e.g., Genesis 4:23. If Genesis were truly poetic, it would use parallelisms throughout.[12]

The mention of "creation accounts" is simply a hint at the defunct "documentary hypothesis," which argued that Genesis was pieced together from several contradictory sources.[13] The charge of contradiction between Genesis 1 and 2 is amply resolved by noting that Genesis 1:1–2:4a is a summary outline of the whole creation, while Genesis 2:4b and the rest of the chapter focuses on the creation of male and female, so they are complementary rather than contradictory.[14]

PBS 7 showed a small segment of an interview with Ken Ham, who says that evolution is an "evil" to be fought and points out the conflicts between the Bible and secular "science" that deals with origins. Then the program showed snippets from a *free* seminar Mr. Ham gave, but deceitfully shows money changing hands at the same time as it shows people entering the auditorium. But the money was either for books, videos, etc., or for

---

12. W.C. Kaiser Jr., "The Literary Form of Genesis 1–11," in J.B. Payne, *New Perspectives on the Old Testament* (Waco, TX: Word, Inc., 1970), p. 59–60.
13. The documentary hypothesis is amply refuted by R. Grigg, "Did Moses Really Write Genesis?" *Creation* 20(4):43–46 (September–November 1998).
14. See D. Batten, "Genesis Contradictions?" *Creation* 18(4):44–45 (September–November 1996).

another seminar (most AiG meetings are free). The PBS program presumably wished to present Christian ministries as "in it for the money."

When PBS showed Mr. Ham presenting arguments against evolution at a seminar, the *omissions* were conspicuous. Cameramen were present for the whole seminar, and they also recorded a two-hour interview with him. But the final cut omitted Mr. Ham's discussion of the key problem for all proponents of evolution or billions of years: the problem of death and suffering before Adam's sin. Ken Ham also presented extensive *scientific* criticisms of evolution in both the seminar and the interview, but these criticisms were omitted. For example, he showed that natural selection and variation, e.g., breeding of dogs, merely involves *sorting* and *loss* of genetic information, while goo-to-you evolution requires *increase* of information.

Presenting this information wouldn't suit the PBS propagandists for two reasons: In general, they wished to portray all objections to evolution as "religious." Of course, they had to ignore the many scientists who are creationists, as well as most of the founders of modern science. Specifically, these points blow most of the PBS program's "evidence" sky high.

Christian college compromise causes confusion!

The damage that evolution has caused on college campuses is legendary, and it's not difficult to cite examples of children from Christian homes who have turned away from their childhood faith after attending college — even "Christian" college. The final episode of the PBS series gives a striking example from Wheaton College, which is said to be a conservative Christian college. According to Wheaton's website:

Wheaton College selects candidates for admission from those who evidence a vital Christian experience, high academic ability, moral character, personal integrity, social concern, and the desire to pursue a liberal arts education as defined in the aims and objectives of the College.

This college is the show-pony of the PBS series, showing viewers how people can mix "God" and evolution. But one must wonder how the school defines a "vital Christian experience" since their professors evidently don't believe the Bible, the only source of information about Christ. At one point in the PBS series, it shows a teacher on a school field trip who proclaims that a water hole is 33 million years old.

There was quite a stir back in 1961 when Prof. Walter Hearn promoted evolution at Wheaton. As a result of this controversy, now the school apparently insists that professors sign a statement that Adam was a historical figure.

But the PBS clips make it abundantly clear that this statement is a dead letter. If the professors themselves "support" this apparent anti-evolution statement, they have no qualms about inviting visiting lecturers who don't believe the biblical account of creation and even attack it.

One example is Keith Miller, who claimed on the PBS program to be an "ardent evangelical Christian." He asserted, without evidence, that there are lots of transitional forms. When questioned, he said that God chose Adam and Eve out of other humans that existed. This just shows that the word "evangelical," like "Christian," has become debased currency. At one time it meant someone who believed the Reformation (and biblical) doctrines of the inerrancy and sufficiency of Scripture. This is not always so nowadays, and certainly doesn't apply to Miller.

Genesis 2:7 teaches that the first man was made from dust and became alive when God breathed the breath of life into him. This rules out the idea that Adam was already a living primate of some kind when God breathed on him. Eve was made from Adam's rib (Gen. 2:21–24). Luke's genealogy of Christ traces His lineage (through Mary) all the way back to Adam, then directly to God, not via any ape-like creatures or pond scum (Luke 3:23–38). Further, 1 Corinthians 15:45 states that Adam was the "first man," and Eve was so named because she was to become the "mother of all living" (Gen. 3:20). Also, Paul's teachings about male and female roles in 1 Corinthians 11:8–9 and 1 Timothy 2:13–14 explicitly support the historical order of creation in Genesis 2:21–23.

The sad thing about Wheaton is the admission — shown on the final PBS episode — that most people become *more* confused about their Christian faith while they attend this "Christian" college. The students wonder whether there's a place for God if evolution is true, and rightly so.[15]

This confusion should hardly be surprising — Billy Graham's former colleague Charles Templeton totally apostatized after attending the compromising Princeton Theological Seminary.[16] Answers in Genesis has received several testimonies of people whose faith was shipwrecked by compromising "Christians" but later restored with the help of AiG and other Christian ministries that present a consistently biblical approach to origins.[17]

15. See John Woodmorappe, "The Horse and the Tractor: Why God and Evolution Don't Mix," *Creation* 22(4):53 (September–November 2000).
16. See K. Ham and S. Byers, "Slippery Slide to Unbelief: A Famous Evangelist Goes from Hope to Hopelessness," *Creation* 22(3):8–13 (June–August 2000).
17. See Sonia's Testimony: "*Creation* Magazine Opened My Eyes to the Gospel!" <www.answersingenesis.org/sonia> and "A Testimony: Joel Galvin," <www.answersingenesis.org/galvin>.

Seeds of apostasy

In contrast to the claims of evolutionists, evolution is a direct assault on the authority of Scripture, and it is the seed of most modern apostasy. Exhibit A is Nathan Baird, a geology major who stars in the final PBS episode. He had a creationist upbringing, sort of, but now from his lofty height at Wheaton he proclaims that most Christians dismiss evolution because they don't understand it. Now he thinks that God used the big bang and evolution, and infused a spirit supernaturally into some humans. He proclaimed: "God is bigger than the box I've put him in."

This slogan is hardly original with Nathan. Rank apostates like retired Episcopal Bishop John Shelby Spong[18] also spout such vacuous tripe. But creationists don't put God into any box; rather, they are humble enough to believe what God has revealed about himself in the Bible, including when and how He created. It's people like Nathan who put God into a box of their own making, by presuming that God would not have intervened in His creation in a different way from the way He currently upholds it (Col. 1:16–17; Hebrews 1:3 — passages referring to Jesus Christ, the God-man). They also, in effect, presume that God was unable to communicate in clear language about the history of the universe.

Lack of apologetics

Nathan's upbringing is sadly typical of the lack of apologetics teaching in the churches. Many Christians have no idea how to defend their faith. The most serious problem is that parents do not have answers to their children's questions.

18. See M. Bott and J. Sarfati, "What's Wrong with Bishop Spong?" *Apologia* 4(1):3–27, 1995; <www.answersingenesis.org/spong>.

PBS 7 showed Nathan's family outside having lunch. Nathan's father correctly believed that evolution was a frontal assault on Genesis 1 and his son's faith, but he didn't seem very well informed about the issues (or else his most telling arguments were edited out, as with AiG). Nathan's father couldn't answer some of his son's facile arguments, and he asked his mother to bail him out.

Nathan's mother correctly pointed out that unwavering adherence to the Bible was a common factor in church growth. She also recounted the advice of a friend: "Don't send Nathan to Wheaton — it could destroy his faith." One might argue whether a person who "loses his/her faith" truly had saving faith to begin with (1 John 2:19), but this incident shows that Wheaton had a reputation for undermining students' faith. It's a shame that Nathan's mother didn't follow this advice before forking out a fortune to a college that doesn't teach what it claims. The money may as well be spent on a secular college, because at least their students know what to expect. It's fortunate for Wheaton and many other "Christian" colleges that they can't be sued for false advertising.

Darwinian evolution truly was a "dangerous idea," one that consciously undermined faith in God and belief in the Bible, replacing it with skepticism and a materialist world view. It's the height of hypocrisy for atheists like Gould to claim that evolution is "compatible" with Christianity.

CHAPTER 3

ARGUMENT: EVOLUTION IS *TRUE* SCIENCE, NOT "JUST A THEORY"

Evolutionists say, "Evolution is real science that
solves real problems; it is founded on the
modern belief that we should try to explain
the universe in natural terms."

Evolutionists bristle at the accusation that evolution is "just a theory," not a fact. Indeed, this is the very first example of "creationist nonsense" that *Scientific American* lists and answers in its "15 Answers to Creationist Nonsense."

1. EVOLUTION IS ONLY A THEORY. IT IS NOT A FACT OR A SCIENTIFIC LAW.

All sciences frequently rely on indirect evidence. Physicists cannot see subatomic particles directly, for instance, so they verify their existence by watching for telltale tracks that the particles leave in cloud chambers. The absence of direct observation does not make physicists' conclusions less certain. [*SA* 79]

Unfortunately, some creationists actually do argue that "evolution is just a theory." What they usually *mean* is "Evolution is not proven fact, so it should not be promoted dogmatically." (Therefore, that is what they *should* say.) The problem with using the word "theory" in this case is that scientists use it to mean a well-substantiated explanation of data. This includes well-known ones such as Einstein's theory of relativity and Newton's theory of gravity, and lesser-known ones such as the Debye–Hückel theory of electrolyte solutions and the Deryagin–Landau/Verwey–Overbeek (DLVO) theory of the stability of lyophobic sols, etc. It would be better to say that particles-to-people evolution is an unsubstantiated *hypothesis* or *conjecture*.

Scientific American's comments about the scientific study of subatomic particles, however, miss the point — these cloud chamber experiments are still *observations* in the *present* and are *repeatable*. A dinosaur turning into a bird 150 Ma (million years ago) is neither observable in real time, directly or indirectly, nor repeatable. Chapter 1 of this book explained this confusion about the difference between "operational science" and "origins science."

WHAT IS SCIENCE? WHAT IS A THEORY?

Scientific American devoted the first *five* points of its article on "creationist nonsense" to defending evolution against charges that it's not good science. In this chapter we will look at each in turn, but first it's absolutely essential to define terms carefully. How can you know whether something is "true science" or "just a theory," unless you know what these terms mean? Yet evolutionists often make sweeping claims without adequately defining their terms.

The 16th century philosopher Sir Francis Bacon, considered the founder of the scientific method, gave a pretty straightforward definition of science:

observation →induction →hypothesis →test hypothesis by experiment →proof/disproof →knowledge.

This view of science, however, depends on two major philosophical assumptions: causality and induction, which must be accepted by faith. Many modern scientists are so ignorant of basic philosophy that they don't even realize they have made these assumptions, although several philosophers, such as David Hume and Bertrand Russell, have pointed it out.[1]

The editors of *Scientific American* and other leading evolutionists define "science" in a self-serving way that excludes God and His Word. They openly equate science with the philosophy of "methological naturalism" — as has already been shown — "to explain the universe purely in terms of observed or testable natural mechanisms." [*SA* 85]

The prominent evolutionary biologist Richard Lewontin has spoken bluntly about this anti-God, materialistic bias:

> We take the side of science *in spite* of the patent absurdity of some of its constructs, *in spite* of its failure to fulfil many of its extravagant promises of health and life, *in spite* of the tolerance of the scientific community for unsubstantiated just-so stories, because we have a prior commitment, a commitment to materialism. It is not that the methods and institutions of science somehow

1. D. Batten, "It's Not Science," <www.answersingenesis.org/not_science>.

compel us to accept a material explanation of the phenomenal world, but, on the contrary, that we are forced by our *a priori* adherence to material causes to create an apparatus of investigation and a set of concepts that produce material explanations, no matter how counter-intuitive, no matter how mystifying to the uninitiated. Moreover, that materialism is an absolute, for we cannot allow a Divine Foot in the door."[2]

Most people think that "science" follows the evidence wherever it leads. But it is impossible to avoid letting our world view color our interpretation of the facts. Creationists are honest about the philosophical basis behind their interpretation, whereas naturalists often pretend that they don't operate from any philosophical bias. The late atheist Stephen Jay Gould, unlike many of his peers, was candid about this bias:

Our ways of learning about the world are strongly influenced by the social preconceptions and biased modes of thinking that each scientist must apply to any problem. The stereotype of a fully rational and objective "scientific method," with individual scientists as logical (and interchangeable) robots is self-serving mythology.[3]

The philosopher of science David Hull had earlier noted:

. . . science is not as empirical as many scientists seem to think it is. Unobserved and even unobservable entities play an important part in it. Science is not just the making of observations: it

2. R. Lewontin, "Billions and Billions of Demons," *New York Review* (January 9, 1997): p. 31; <www.answersingenesis.org/lewontin>.
3. S.J. Gould, *Natural History* 103(2):14, 1994.

is the making of inferences on the basis of observations within the framework of a theory.[4]

Dr. Scott Todd, an immunologist at Kansas State University, was candid about how certain conclusions would be avoided at all costs, regardless of the evidence:

> Even if all the data point to an intelligent designer, such an hypothesis is excluded from science because it is not naturalistic.[5]

WHAT IS EVOLUTION?

It is vitally important that words such as "evolution" be used accurately and consistently. The theory of "evolution" that the evolutionists are really promoting, and which creationists oppose, is the idea that particles turned into people over time, without any need for an intelligent Designer. The evolutionist Kerkut accurately defined this "general theory of evolution" (GTE) as "the theory that all the living forms in the world have arisen from a single source which itself came from an inorganic form." He continued: "The evidence which supports this is not sufficiently strong to allow us to consider it as anything more than a working hypothesis."[6]

However, many evolutionary propagandists are guilty of the deceitful practice of *equivocation*, that is, switching the meaning of a single word (evolution) part way through an argument. A common tactic, "bait-and-switch," is simply to produce examples of change over time, call this "evolution," then imply that the GTE is thereby proven or even essential, and creation disproved.

4. D. Hull, "The Effect of Essentialism on Taxonomy — Two Thousand Years of Stasis (II)," *British Journal for the Philosophy of Science* 16(61):1–18, 1965.
5. S.C. Todd, correspondence to *Nature* 410(6752):423 (September 30, 1999); <www.answersingenesis.org/todd>.
6. G.A. Kerkut, *Implications of Evolution* (Oxford, UK: Pergamon, 1960), p. 157.

The PBS "Evolution" series and the *Scientific American* article are full of examples of this fallacy.

Information — the real problem with evolution

The main scientific objection to the GTE is *not* that changes occur through time, and neither is it about the *size* of the change (so I would discourage use of the terms micro- and macro-evolution — see the appendix to this book). The key issue is the *type* of change required — to change microbes into men requires changes that *increase the genetic information content*. The three billion DNA "letters" stored in each human cell nucleus convey a great deal more information (known as "specified complexity") than the over half a million DNA "letters" of the "simplest" self-reproducing organism. The DNA sequences in a "higher" organism, such as a human being or a horse, for instance, code for structures and functions unknown in the sort of "primitive first cell" from which all other organisms are said to have evolved.

None of the alleged proofs of "evolution in action" provide a *single* example of functional new information being added to genes. Rather, they all involve sorting and loss of information. To claim that mere change proves that information-*increasing* change can occur is like saying that because a merchant can sell goods, he can sell them for a profit. The origin of information is a major problem for the GTE.[7] "Information theory," as it is called, is a whole new branch of science that has effectively destroyed the last underpinnings of evolution — explained fully in the monumental work *In the Beginning Was Information* by Dr. Werner Gitt, professor and head

---

7. See C. Wieland, "Beetle Bloopers," *Creation* 19(3):30 (June–August 1997); K. Ham, "How Would You Answer?" *Creation* 20(3):32–34 (June–August 1998); and R. Grigg, "Information: A Modern Scientific Design Argument," *Creation* 22(2):50–53 (March–May 2000).

of the Department of Information Technology at the German Federal Institute of Physics and Technology.

The second episode of the PBS *Evolution* series, titled "Great Transformations," faced this problem when it tried to prove the "big picture" of evolution, i.e., the "general theory of evolution." Of course, it could offer no experimental evidence, only inference. Its only experimental "evidence" for "evolution" was a bunch of examples of biological change that don't increase information content, and so actually these examples have nothing to do with the "big picture."

The PBS program did make a revealing comment about the real nature of the "evidence" for evolution: "The evidence for evolution is all around us, if we choose to look for it." The comment is revealing, not because the evidence really supports evolution, but because the narrator inadvertently makes an important point. That is, creationists and evolutionists have the same evidence (facts), but we interpret it differently because of our different axioms (starting assumptions). In reality, evolutionists have a materialistic bias, which rejects a common Designer *a priori* (see Lewontin's admission earlier in this chapter), and this applies even to evolutionists who believe in "God." Because of their bias, evolutionists interpret *any* facts as evidence for evolution. This would probably explain why a lot of the science in the PBS series was not even directly stated as evidence for evolution, but is shown as if it is. It also explains why fragmentary remains are interpreted as important "transitional forms." Conversely, creationists do *not* dispute the facts, since we have the same facts, although we frequently dispute assertions *claimed* to be facts when they are certainly not!

The PBS narrator blindly asserts that all living organisms come from a single source and that we can now trace branches and roots. Yet the series utterly fails to explain one of the most vexing problems with evolution: how non-living chemicals could form a living cell by time and chance, despite the insuperable chemical hurdles.[8] Interestingly, the PBS producer Richard Hutton never acknowledged this problem in the series, but he did on a *Washington Post* online forum, when he answered the question "What are some of the larger questions which are still unanswered by evolutionary theory?"

> There are open questions and controversies, and the fights can be fierce. Just a few of them: The origin of life. There is no consensus at all here — lots of theories, little science. That's one of the reasons we didn't cover it in the series. The evidence wasn't very good.[9]

No, the evidence for the first living organism certainly isn't "very good" (see chapter 9), but of course the producer wouldn't want his viewers to know that! In other words, the very roots of the alleged evolutionary tree are in very bad shape. So they gloss over the problems, assert that there really is a well-documented tree, and then move on to find similarities between organisms and claim that this proves a common ancestor.

SWATTING AT GNATS

Instead of properly defining evolution or addressing the key scientific problem with evolution — i.e., the miraculous appearance of new genetic information from

8. See also C.B. Thaxton, W.L. Bradley, and R.L. Olsen, *The Mystery of Life's Origin* (New York, NY: Philosophical Library Inc., 1984); <www.answersingenesis.org/origin>.

9. http://discuss.washingtonpost.com/wp-srv/zforum/01/evolution2_092601.htm, last downloaded September 1, 2002.

nothing — evolutionists swat at gnats and swallow camels. Just look at the second and third examples of "creationist nonsense" in *Scientific American*'s "15 Answers to Creationist Nonsense." Both of them miss the point.

2. NATURAL SELECTION IS BASED ON CIRCULAR REASONING: THE FITTEST ARE THOSE WHO SURVIVE, AND THOSE WHO SURVIVE ARE DEEMED FITTEST. [*SA* 79]

Like the creationist argument that evolution is "just a theory," this is another argument that Answers in Genesis has previously advised creationists not to use (see the appendix to this book). Why should we argue this, since tautology is quite common in science? Moreover, as will be shown in detail in the next chapter, natural selection is *not* evidence of evolution. In fact, it is an important part of the creation/Fall framework!

3. EVOLUTION IS UNSCIENTIFIC, BECAUSE IT IS NOT TESTABLE OR FALSIFIABLE. IT MAKES CLAIMS ABOUT EVENTS THAT WERE NOT OBSERVED AND CAN NEVER BE RE-CREATED.

This blanket dismissal of evolution ignores important distinctions that divide the field into at least two broad areas: microevolution and macroevolution. Microevolution looks at changes within species over time — changes that may be preludes to speciation, the origin of new species. Macroevolution studies how taxonomic groups above the level of species change. Its evidence draws frequently from the fossil record and DNA comparisons to reconstruct how various organisms may be related. [*SA* 80]

Look who's talking about "ignoring important distinctions"! It's evolutionary propagandists who generally mix them up. Biologists frequently define evolution as "change in gene frequency with time" or "descent with modification," or other such "*micro*evolution" words, and then cite insignificant examples of change within species, such as Darwin's finches, as clinching proof of "evolution" in the "*macro*" sense and disproof of creationism! An example is Eugenie Scott, who approvingly cited a teacher whose pupils said after her "definition," "*Of course* species change with time! You mean that's evolution?!*"[10]

Glossing over the absence of evidence

With such verbal sleights of hand, evolutionists gloss over their complete lack of evidence for so-called "macroevolution." Their supposed "evidence" doesn't speak for itself; it must be *interpreted*. As John Rennie admitted in *Scientific American*, this evidence is interpreted within a materialistic framework. Ironically, materialists turn around and proclaim evolution as a major evidence for materialism, even though their materialistic framework was responsible for this viewpoint in the first place! Creationists interpret the same evidence but by a biblical framework, and they reach opposite conclusions.[11]

Another supposed "evidence" that evolution makes good science is its ability to make "predictions about future discoveries," such as the discovery of "a succession of hominid creatures with features progressively less apelike and more modern."[12] *Scientific American* makes this very claim.

In the historical sciences (which include astronomy, geology, and archaeology, as well as

---

10. E. Scott, "Dealing with Anti-evolutionism," *Reports of the National Center for Science Education* (4):24–28, 1997; quote on p. 26, with emphasis in original.
11. See K. Ham, "Creation: 'Where's the Proof?' " *Creation* 22(1):39–42 (December 1999–February 2000).
12. The false claim of transitional forms between apes and humans is discussed in chapter 12.

evolutionary biology), hypotheses can still be tested by checking whether they accord with physical evidence and whether they lead to verifiable predictions about future discoveries. For instance, evolution implies that between the earliest-known ancestors of humans (roughly five million years old) and the appearance of anatomically modern humans (about 100,000 years ago), one should find a succession of hominid creatures with features progressively less apelike and more modern, which is indeed what the fossil record shows. . . . Evolutionary biology [also] routinely makes predictions far more refined and precise than this, and researchers test them constantly. [*SA* 80]

Given such flimsy evidence for the scientific integrity of evolution, what "evidence" would be required to disprove evolution (an especially difficult task, because it is impossible to "disprove" a philosophical assumption)? *Scientific American* tries, anyway.

Evolution could be disproved in other ways, too. If we could document the spontaneous generation of just one complex life-form from inanimate matter, then at least a few creatures seen in the fossil record might have originated this way. If superintelligent aliens appeared and claimed credit for creating life on earth (or even particular species), the purely evolutionary explanation would be cast in doubt. But no one has yet produced such evidence. [*SA* 80]

None of this would "disprove evolution," since big-picture evolution is really just a grab bag of ideas about naturalistic (God-less) origins. Evolutionists already believe in spontaneous generation, but now call it "chemical evolution." They would actually be *delighted* if any or multiple examples of spontaneous generation were documented, because it would vindicate their belief that life came into being without an intelligent Creator. It would also solve their problem with the DNA in microbes, which does not show a pattern consistent with the presumption that it shares a common ancestry with other forms of life. To solve this vexing problem, multiple spontaneous origins have already been proposed, without any suggestion that this would "disprove evolution."[13]

The Bible claims to be a revelation by the Creator of life and the universe, who certainly has "claimed credit for creating life on earth," yet *Scientific American* editor John Rennie does not see this as casting doubt on evolution. And there is excellent historical, archaeological, and textual evidence that the Bible's claims are true.[14] But Rennie has apparently already made up his mind that this evidence doesn't exist — this would presumably upset his materialistic faith. He goes on to say,

> It should be noted that the idea of falsifiability as the defining characteristic of science originated with philosopher Karl Popper in the 1930s. More recent elaborations on his thinking have expanded the narrowest interpretation of his principle precisely because it would eliminate too many branches of clearly scientific endeavor. [*SA* 80]

This is simply an attempt to immunize evolution from the same criticism that is advanced against creationists.

---

13. A. Barnett, "The Second Coming. Did Life Evolve on Earth More Than Once?" *New Scientist* 157(2121):19, 1998.
14. See <www.answersingenesis.org/bible>.

A "GOOD THEORY" BECAUSE IT'S "WIDELY ACCEPTED"?

One of the most absurd, self-serving criteria that evolutionists give for a good scientific theory is that most published scientists accept the theory as valid. This is the basis for *Scientific American*'s next attack on "creationist nonsense."

4. INCREASINGLY, SCIENTISTS DOUBT THE TRUTH OF EVOLUTION.

No evidence suggests that evolution is losing adherents. Pick up any issue of a peer-reviewed biological journal, and you will find articles that support and extend evolutionary studies or that embrace evolution as a fundamental concept.

Conversely, serious scientific publications disputing evolution are all but nonexistent. In the mid-1990s George W. Gilchrist of the University of Washington surveyed thousands of journals in the primary literature, seeking articles on intelligent design or creation science. Among those hundreds of thousands of scientific reports, he found none. In the past two years, surveys done independently by Barbara Forrest of Southeastern Louisiana University and Lawrence M. Krauss of Case Western Reserve University have been similarly fruitless. [*SA* 80]

It's logically possible for a belief to lose adherents even if journals still publish articles supporting this belief. Scientists who base such wild claims on a review of journals might benefit from some study of simple logic.[15]

Do they even know what to look for? Creationists are hardly likely to want to blow their cover and risk the discrimination epitomized by *Scientific American*. Would *Nature* or *Science,* for example, ever knowingly publish a paper favorable to creation? Hardly. But in spite of the bias against such publication, creationist scientists have managed to publish papers when the creationist implications are disguised subtly enough. This shows that they *do* carry out real scientific research. Yet "15 Answers to Creationist Nonsense" has the audacity to claim:

> Creationists retort that a closed-minded scientific community rejects their evidence. Yet according to the editors of *Nature, Science,* and other leading journals, few antievolution manuscripts are even submitted. [*SA* 80][16]

An absolutely amazing comment coming from a journal that's publicly reached the nadir of anti-creationist censorship and discrimination!

There is clear proof of censorship by *Scientific American*, *Science,* and *Australasian Science*, where they have even denied creationists the normal courtesy of the right of reply. So why would scientists bother to waste their time? They know that their papers will be rejected, no matter how good the research, which explains why creationist scientists have, years ago, commenced their own peer-reviewed journals. *Scientific American* acknowledges the credentials of some creationists, but not the fanatical censorship that they face.

15. J.D. Sarfati, "Loving God with All Your Mind: Logic and Creation," *TJ* 12(2):142–151 (1998).
16. Examples are listed in D. Buckna, "Do Creationists Publish in Notable Refereed Journals?" <http://www.answersingenesis.org/docs/538.asp>.

Some anti-evolution authors have published papers in serious journals. Those papers, however, rarely attack evolution directly or advance creationist arguments; at best, they identify certain evolutionary problems as unsolved and difficult (which no one disputes).

An interesting admission, but that's hardly the impression that evolutionists usually give to the public.

In short, creationists are not giving the scientific world good reason to take them seriously. [*SA* 80]

So why does *Scientific American* take us seriously by writing this article?

"DISAGREEMENTS AREN'T DOUBTS ABOUT EVOLUTION" — DOUBLETALK

Scientific American's next example of supposed "creationist nonsense" turns out to be doubletalk, and merely closes ranks against creationists. It repeats the old trick of claiming "there is no doubt that evolution occurred; the only disagreement is about the mechanism."

5. THE DISAGREEMENTS AMONG EVEN EVOLUTIONARY BIOLOGISTS SHOW HOW LITTLE SOLID SCIENCE SUPPORTS EVOLUTION.

Evolutionary biologists passionately debate diverse topics: how speciation happens, the rates of evolutionary change, the ancestral relationships of birds and dinosaurs, whether Neandertals were a species apart from modern humans, and much more. These disputes are like those found in all other branches of science. Acceptance of evolution as a factual occurrence and a guiding principle is nonetheless universal in biology. [*SA* 81]

This rhetorical flourish notwithstanding, modern evolutionary theory is *all about* providing a plausible mechanism for explaining life's complexity without God. If the disputes undermine all the favored mechanisms for evolution, then the whole materialist apologetic crumbles. When the supporters of various evolutionary camps score mortal blows against the mechanisms proposed by their rival camps, it's perfectly reasonable for creationists to point this out.

For example, with the origin of birds, there are two main theories: that birds evolved "ground up" from running dinosaurs (the *cursorial* theory), and that they evolved "trees down" from small reptiles (the *arboreal* theory). Both sides produce devastating arguments against the other side. The evidence indicates that the critics are *both* right — birds did not evolve either from running dinosaurs or from tree-dwelling mini-crocodiles. In fact, birds did not evolve from non-birds at all!

Similarly, supporters of "jerky" evolution (*saltationism* and its relative, *punctuated equilibria*) point out that the fossil record does not show gradualism, and that the hypothetical transitional forms would be disadvantageous. But supporters of gradual evolution point out that sudden, large, information-increasing change is so improbable that one would need to invoke a secular "miracle." Creationists agree with both sides: punctuated evolution can't happen, and gradual evolution can't happen — in fact, particles-to-people evolution can't happen at all!

Lacking sound arguments, *Scientific American* stoops to quipping,

> Unfortunately, dishonest creationists have shown a willingness to take scientists' comments out of context to exaggerate and distort the disagreements. [*SA* 81]

Pure assertion. This "quoting out of context" assertion is a common misrepresentation repeated by skeptics and their church allies. An even sillier thing is to write to an author and ask whether he had been misquoted, which some anti-creationists actually do, as surprising as it may seem. All one needs to do to demonstrate misquoting is to compare the quote with the original.

The most frequently cited example of creationists "misquoting" an avid evolutionist is their handling of Gould's punctuated equilibrium model. *Scientific American* says:

> Anyone acquainted with the works of paleontologist Stephen Jay Gould of Harvard University knows that in addition to co-authoring the punctuated-equilibrium model, Gould was one of the most eloquent defenders and articulators of evolution. (Punctuated equilibrium explains patterns in the fossil record by suggesting that most evolutionary changes occur within geologically brief intervals — which may nonetheless amount to hundreds of generations.) Yet creationists delight in dissecting out phrases from Gould's voluminous prose to make him sound as though he had doubted evolution. . . . [*SA* 81]

Creationists do no such thing. Rather, they make it very clear that Gould was a staunch evolutionist but he criticized many aspects of neo-Darwinian theory. Quoting Gould is the perfectly honorable strategy of using a hostile witness.[17]

Yet *Scientific American* continues the misrepresentation of creationist claims:

---

17. See Don Batten, "Did Creationists 'Hijack' Gould's Idea?" *TJ* 16(2):22–24, 2002; <www.answersingenesis.org/gould>.

. . . and they present punctuated equilibrium as though it allows new species to materialize overnight or birds to be born from reptile eggs. [*SA* 81]

First, most creationists present Gould's ideas correctly, and those ideas are not the exclusive property of evolutionists. Second, even many evolutionists think that Gould has largely himself to blame because of his injudicious (from an evolutionary viewpoint) comments. For example, Richard Goldschmidt was famous for promoting a "hopeful monster" theory, which indeed said something very much like a bird hatching from a reptile egg. And Gould wrote an article called "The Return of Hopeful Monsters," which said:

I do, however, predict that during the next decade Goldschmidt will be largely vindicated in the world of evolutionary biology.[18]

If there is any "out-of-context" quote in any books or articles written by me or my colleagues, we would like to know about it, because we are not about misleading people. Where such things have very rarely occurred in our literature over the years, we have willingly corrected them. *Scientific American* ends this discussion of this type of "creationist nonsense" with yet another sweeping assertion, but without substance.

When confronted with a quotation from a scientific authority that seems to question evolution, insist on seeing the statement in context. Almost invariably, the attack on evolution will prove illusory. [*SA* 81]

---

18. S.J. Gould, "The Return of Hopeful Monsters," *Natural History* 86(6):22–30, 1977.

In reality, experience shows that when confronted by an accusation against creation or creationists by any scientific "authority," one should insist on seeing documentation. Almost invariably, the attack on creation will prove illusory.

ELEPHANT HURLING

There is a debate tactic known as "elephant hurling." This occurs when the critic throws summary arguments about complex issues to give the impression of weighty evidence, but with an unstated presumption that a large complex of underlying ideas is true, and failing to consider opposing data, usually because they have uncritically accepted the arguments from their own side. But we should challenge elephant-hurlers to offer *specifics* and challenge the *underlying assumptions*.

John Rennie's article on "15 Answers to Creationist Nonsense" opens with a classic example of elephant hurling.

> When Charles Darwin introduced the theory of evolution through natural selection 143 years ago, the scientists of the day argued over it fiercely, but the massing evidence from paleontology, genetics, zoology, molecular biology, and other fields gradually established evolution's truth beyond reasonable doubt. Today that battle has been won everywhere — except in the public imagination. [*SA* 78]

It is true that Darwin faced intense opposition when he introduced evolution. But his main opposition came from the *scientists*[19] and much of his support came from compromising clergymen, such as Rev. Charles Kingsley,

---

19. See J. Foard, "Holy War? Who Really Opposed Darwin?" *Creation* 21(4):26–27 (September–November 1999).

who applied it to humans to assert that the African-Americans and Australian Aborigines had not evolved enough to understand the gospel.[20]

To be honest, I think *Scientific American* underestimates the hold of evolution on the "public imagination." While many Americans say they believe in creation and reject evolution, sadly many seem to be "evolutionized" in their thinking. This is shown by the widespread idea that their personal faith should not influence their public life. It's unfortunate to hear professing Christians who say that they won't let their faith influence their public policy, e.g., "I'm personally opposed to abortion, but I won't enforce my faith on the pregnant woman who must be given the right to choose," although the unborn baby has no "choice." However, atheists are very happy to let their own faith influence their public policy and enforce their views on people — we rarely hear: "I'm personally in favor of abortion, but I won't enforce my view on the innocent unborn baby."[21]

For this reason, the primary focus of Christian apologetics ministries like Answers in Genesis is not on refuting evolution *per se*, which by itself will accomplish little to change lives and opinions, but rather building a consistent biblical Christian world view. Refuting evolution (and millions of years) is a corollary.[22]

Scientific American's "elephant hurling" continues with a repeat of common *ad hominem* attacks on the intelligence of creationists and their imagined threat to the advances of "modern science" (as evolution is claimed to be):

---

20. See R. Grigg, "Darwin's Quisling," *Creation* 22 (1):50–51 (December 1999–February 2000).
21. The related fallacy that "you cannot/should not legislate morality" has been refuted in many articles, such as Michael Bauman, "Dispelling False Notions of the First Amendment: The Falsity, Futility, Folly of Separating Morality from Law," <http://www.equip.org/free/DM801.htm>, Christian Research Institute.
22. C. Wieland, AiG's views on the Intelligent Design Movement, www.answersingenesis.org/IDM, August 30, 2002.

Embarrassingly, in the 21st century, in the most scientifically advanced nation the world has ever known, creationists can still persuade politicians, judges, and ordinary citizens that evolution is a flawed, poorly supported fantasy. They lobby for creationist ideas such as "intelligent design" to be taught as alternatives to evolution in science classrooms. [*SA* 78]

Perhaps the United States is "the most scientifically advanced nation the world has ever known" precisely because it has been the most Bible-based society the world has ever known! And that includes belief in the biblical account of creation, the Fall and the Flood.[23]

Again, AiG is not a lobby group, and it opposes legislation for *compulsion* of creation teaching. But there is nothing wrong with giving legal protection to teachers who want to present scientific arguments against the sacred cow of evolution. Yet *Scientific American* and the intelligentsia are mortified by the possibility:

As this article goes to press, the Ohio Board of Education is debating whether to mandate such a change. Some anti-evolutionists, such as Philip E. Johnson, a law professor at the University of California at Berkeley and author of *Darwin on Trial,* admit that they intend for intelligent-design theory to serve as a "wedge" for reopening science classrooms to discussions of God. [*SA* 78]

Horrors, discuss God in the classroom? By this "reasoning," John Rennie would have to blast Rufus Porter, a believer in biblical creation, who founded his own journal *Scientific American* for a similar purpose!

---

23. See "The Creationist Basis for Modern Science," <http://www.answersingenesis.org/docs/270.asp>.

Rennie acknowledges the difficulty in answering creationists in the classroom, yet he slams their integrity:

> Besieged teachers and others may increasingly find themselves on the spot to defend evolution and refute creationism. The arguments that creationists use are typically specious and based on misunderstandings of (or outright lies about) evolution, but the number and diversity of the objections can put even well-informed people at a disadvantage. [*SA* 78]

Is it possible that the "well-informed" find the creationist arguments convincing because they recognize the validity of them? And most real scientists whom *Scientific American* would call "well-informed" actually have no use for evolution in their work!

Yet Rennie believes it is his duty to do his very best to shore up the cause of the embattled evolutionists with his cover story on "creationist nonsense."

> To help with answering them, the following list rebuts some of the most common "scientific" arguments raised against evolution. It also directs readers to further sources for information and explains why creation science has no place in the classroom. [*SA* 79]

By heaping together the best "science" of evolutionists to "rebut" creation, *Scientific American* has actually done us all a favor. The remaining chapters of this book will show, in detail, how weak the "best" arguments are, buttressing believers and challenging unbelievers to reconsider their assumptions about the validity of evolutionist propaganda.

2

CLAIM: EVOLUTION IS WELL SUPPORTED BY THE EVIDENCE

Evolutionists claim that they have found abundant, observable evidence of evolution.

CHAPTER 4

ARGUMENT: NATURAL SELECTION LEADS TO SPECIATION

Evolutionists say, "Natural selection has been observed to cause profound changes in populations — providing abundant evidence for speciation."

GALÁPAGOS FINCHES — EVOLUTION IN ACTION?

The opening episode of the PBS "Evolution" series makes much of the Galápagos finches — considered one of the classic evidences of "evolution in action." But PBS admits that Darwin didn't even realize that the birds were finches and he failed to label which island they came from. All the same, he managed to acquire this information, and he eventually concluded that they had descended from mainland finches with modification — just as the biblical creation/Fall/Flood/migration model would predict! He correctly realized that finch beak size was the result of adaptation to different food sources.

The problem is that Darwin and the PBS series taught that this adaptation could explain the general theory of evolution. But the finch beak variation is merely the result of selection of *existing* genetic information, while the GTE requires *new* information. Also, an 18-year study by zoologist Peter Grant showed that a new species could arise in only 200 years,[1] which is inadvertent support for the biblical model of rapid speciation.[2] However, another problem with using these finches is that the variation seems to be cyclic — while a drought resulted in a slight increase in beak size, the change was reversed when the rains returned. So it looks more like *built-in* adaptability to various climatic conditions than anything to do with the GTE.

PBS also discusses the change in beak length of hummingbirds, to adapt to changes in the lengths of flowers where they obtain nectar. But the same points apply — no evidence was produced that any new information is required for these changes, as opposed to selection of already-existing information.

WHAT IS THE BIBLICAL CREATIONIST MODEL?

Perhaps the most frequently repeated mistake that evolutionists make in their attacks on creation is to assert that "natural selection" and "speciation" prove evolution

---

1. P.R. Grant, "Natural Selection and Darwin's Finches," *Scientific American* 265(4):60–65 (October 1991).
2. See C. Wieland, "Darwin's Finches: Evidence Supporting Rapid Post-Flood Adaptation," *Creation* 14(3):22–23 (June–August 1992).

and disprove the biblical account of origins. Their bait-and-switch arguments imply that creationists believe in "fixity of species." The glossary for the PBS "Evolution" series *Online Course for Teachers: Teaching Evolution* explicitly makes this empty allegation:

> In creationism, species are described as "fixed" in the sense that they are believed not to change their form, or appearance, through time.

But no reputable creationist denies speciation — in fact, it is an important part of creationist biology. In the previous chapter, I showed that the real issue is whether evolution can explain the *increase of genetic information content* — enough changes to turn microbes into men, *not* simple change through time. Before laying to rest the evolutionists' pointless arguments on this issue, it might be helpful to review the creationist model in detail.

Biblical "kinds" are not modern species

Creationists, starting from the Bible, believe that God created different *kinds* of organisms, which reproduced "after their kinds" (Gen. 1:11, 12, 21, 24, 25). Thus the biblical kinds would have *originally* been distinct biological species, i.e., a population of organisms that can interbreed to produce fertile offspring but that cannot so breed with a different biological species.

But creationists point out that the biblical "kind" is larger than one of *today's* "species." Each of the original kinds was created with a vast amount of information. God made sure that the original creatures had enough variety in their genetic information so that their descendants could adapt to a wide variety of environments.

Based on the biblical criterion for kinds, creationists have made several deductions about the modern descendants of the original creations. They deduce, for example, that as long as two modern creatures can hybridize with true fertilization, the two creatures are descended from the same kind.[3] Also, if two creatures can hybridize with the same third creature, they are all members of the same kind.[4] The hybridization criterion is a valid *operational definition,* which could *in principle* enable researchers to list all the kinds. The implication is one-way — hybridization is evidence that two creatures *are* the same kind, but it does *not* necessarily follow that if hybridization *cannot* occur then they are *not* members of the same kind (failure to hybridize could be due to degenerative mutations). After all, there are couples who can't have children, and we don't classify them as a different species, let alone a different kind.

The boundaries of the "kind" do not always correspond to any given man-made classification such as "species," genus, family, etc. But this is not the fault of the biblical term "kind"; it is actually due to inconsistencies in the man-made classification system. That is, several organisms classified as different "species," and even different genera or higher groupings, can produce fertile offspring. This means that they are really the same species that has several varieties, hence a *polytypic* (many type) species. A good example is Kekaimalu the wholphin, a fertile hybrid between a male false killer whale (*Pseudorca crassidens*) and a female bottlenose dolphin (*Tursiops truncatus*), i.e., between two different so-called *genera.*[5] There are more examples in reference 3.

---

3. F.L. Marsh, *Variation and Fixity in Nature* (Mountain View, CA: Pacific Press, 1976), p. 37.
4. Wm. A. Dembski, *Mere Creation: Science, Faith and Intelligent Design,* "Basic Types of Life," by S. Scherer (Downers Grove, IL: InterVarsity Press, 1998), p. 197.
5. D. Batten, "Ligers and Wholphins? What Next?" *Creation* 22(3):28–33 (June–August 2000).

Biologists have identified several ways that a loss of genetic information through mutations (copying mistakes) can lead to new species — e.g., the loss of a protein's ability to recognize "imprinting" marks, "jumping genes," natural selection, and genetic drift. When these mutations take place in small populations, they can sometimes result in sterile or nonviable offspring. Or changes in song or color might result in birds that no longer recognize a mate, so they no longer interbreed. Either way, a new "species" is formed. Thus, each created kind may have been the ancestor of several present-day species.

But again, it's important to stress that speciation has nothing to do with *real* evolution (GTE), because it involves *sorting* and *loss* of genetic information, rather than *new* information.

The Biblical model predicts *rapid* speciation

The biblical creation/Fall/Flood/migration model would also predict *rapid* formation of new varieties and even species. This is because all the modern varieties of land vertebrates must have descended from comparatively few animals that disembarked from the ark only around 4,500 years ago. In contrast, Darwin thought that this process would normally take eons. It turns out that the very evidence claimed by evolutionists to support their theory supports the biblical model.

Biologists have identified several instances of rapid adaptation, including guppies on Trinidad, lizards in the Bahamas, daisies on the islands of British Columbia, and house mice on Madeira.[6] Another good example is a new "species" of mosquito that can't interbreed with

---

6. D. Catchpoole and C. Wieland, "Speedy Species Surprise," *Creation* 23(2):13–15 (March–May 2001).

the parent population, arising in the London Underground train system (the "Tube") in only 100 years. The rapid change has "astonished" evolutionists, but should delight creationists.[7] *Scientific American* admits as much.

> These days even most creationists acknowledge that microevolution has been upheld by tests in the laboratory (as in studies of cells, plants and fruit flies) and in the field (as in Grant's studies of evolving beak shapes among Galápagos finches). [*SA* 80]

And why should creationists deny such things? All of this so-called microevolution is part of a created and fallen world, but has never been observed to add new genetic information. In fact, the sorts of changes which are observed are the wrong type to drive the evolutionary story.[8] *Scientific American* is forced to make a pointless claim about evidence of "profound" changes:

> Natural selection and other mechanisms — such as chromosomal changes, symbiosis, and hybridization — can drive profound changes in populations over time. [*SA* 80]

Again, do these profound changes *increase information*? No — populations are seen *losing* information, and adapting within the constraints of the information they already have. In contrast, goo-to-you evolution requires something quite different — the progressive addition of massive amounts of genetic information that is *novel* not only to that population, but to the entire biosphere.

---

7. See C. Wieland, "Brisk Biters," *Creation* 21(2):41 (March–May 1999).
8. See C. Wieland, "The Evolution Train's A-coming," *Creation* 24(2) (March–May 2002).

STRAW MAN 1: NATURAL SELECTION CAN'T EXPLAIN NEW SPECIES

Scientific American falls for the same straw-man argument as PBS, failing to recognize that creationists accept new species arising within the kind. Creationists recognize how reproductive isolation can result from information loss. (See discussion above.)

11. NATURAL SELECTION MIGHT EXPLAIN MICRO-EVOLUTION, BUT IT CANNOT EXPLAIN THE ORIGIN OF NEW SPECIES AND HIGHER ORDERS OF LIFE.

Evolutionary biologists have written extensively about how natural selection could produce new species. For instance, in the model called allopatry, developed by Ernst Mayr of Harvard University, if a population of organisms were isolated from the rest of its species by geographical boundaries, it might be subjected to different selective pressures. Changes would accumulate in the isolated population. If those changes became so significant that the splinter group could not or routinely would not breed with the original stock, then the splinter group would be *reproductively isolated* and on its way toward becoming a new species. [*SA* 82]

Indeed, creationists point out that Mayr's allopatric model would explain the origin of the different people groups ("races") after the confusion of languages at Babel induced small population groups to spread out all over the earth.[9] Of course, the modern people groups are *not* reproductively isolated and are still a single biological species.

9. The human "races" issue is covered more fully in chapter 18 of Ken Ham, Andrew Snelling, and Carl Wieland, *The Answers Book* (Green Forest, AR: Master Books, 1990).

Creationists also point out that the mountainous topography of the ark's landing place would be ideal for geographical isolation. This would allow much post-Flood diversification from comparatively few (~8,000) kinds of land vertebrates, by splitting up the original high genetic variation.

Note that the reproductive isolation is an informationally negative change, even if beneficial, because it blocks the interchange of genetic information between populations.

Evolutionists brag that natural selection is the best studied of the evolutionary mechanisms, but these studies show that it has nothing to do with evolution of more complex life forms! All we observe it doing is *removing* information, not adding it. *Scientific American* suggests that there are other feasible mechanisms to explain evolution, but they do not hold up, either.

> Natural selection is the best studied of the evolutionary mechanisms, but biologists are open to other possibilities as well. Biologists are constantly assessing the potential of unusual genetic mechanisms for causing speciation or for producing complex features in organisms. Lynn Margulis of the University of Massachusetts at Amherst and others have persuasively argued that some cellular organelles, such as the energy-generating mitochondria, evolved through the symbiotic merger of ancient organisms. [*SA* 82]

The *endosymbiosis* theory has many problems, such as the lack of evidence that prokaryotes are capable of ingesting another cell and keeping it alive, and the large differences in genes between mitochondria and prokaryotes.[10]

Scientific American admits that it's open to any other mechanism to explain nature — *as long as it excludes God!*

Thus, science welcomes the possibility of evolution resulting from forces beyond natural selection. Yet those forces must be natural; they cannot be attributed to the actions of mysterious creative intelligences whose existence, in scientific terms, is unproved. [*SA* 82]

We have already cited more honest admissions by evolutionists Lewontin and Todd about their *a priori* rejection of a Designer before even examining the evidence. But evolutionary propaganda for public consumption persists in claiming that evolution is accepted purely on scientific grounds.

STRAW MAN 2: EVOLUTIONISTS HAVE SEEN SPECIES EVOLVE

Scientific American tries to make hay with this straw man, devoting *two* points to "proving" natural selection and speciation. Informed creationists don't teach against these biological processes — even though some "day-age" advocates, like Hugh Ross, do.[11]

12. NOBODY HAS EVER SEEN A NEW SPECIES EVOLVE.

Speciation is probably fairly rare and in many cases might take centuries. [*SA* 82]

It might take centuries, but it *need* not. In fact, speciation can happen much faster than most evolutionists (and day-age advocates) realize. Creationists following the

---

10 . See D. Batten, "Did Cells Acquire Organelles Such as Mitochondria by Gobbling Up Other Cells?" < www.answersingenesis.org/endosymbiont >.

11. See <www.answersingenesis.org/ross_YvO>.

biblical creation/Fall/Flood/migration model expect such rapid *non-evolutive* speciation, as we pointed out earlier.

Furthermore, recognizing a new species during a formative stage can be difficult, because biologists sometimes disagree about how best to define a species. The most widely used definition, Mayr's Biological Species Concept, recognizes a species as a distinct community of reproductively isolated populations — sets of organisms that normally do not or cannot breed outside their community. In practice, this standard can be difficult to apply to organisms isolated by distance or terrain or to plants (and, of course, fossils do not breed). Biologists therefore usually use organisms' physical and behavioral traits as clues to their species membership. [*SA* 82]

We agree. It's important to note this difficulty in defining "species" whenever evolutionists claim that creationists don't have a consistent definition of "kinds" (which we do, as discussed before). We also agree with *Scientific American*'s recognition of recent experiments that have caused artificial speciation.

Nevertheless, the scientific literature does contain reports of apparent speciation events in plants, insects, and worms. In most of these experiments, researchers subjected organisms to various types of selection — for anatomical differences, mating behaviors, habitat preferences, and other traits — and found that they had created populations of organisms that did not breed with outsiders. For example, William R. Rice of the University of New Mexico and George W. Salt of the University of California at Davis demonstrated that if they sorted a group of fruit flies by their preference for certain environments and bred those flies separately over 35 generations, the resulting flies would refuse to breed with those from a very different environment. [*SA* 82–83]

None of this is news to informed creationists. Once again, there is no new information, but sorting and loss of already existing information.

ECOLOGY PROVES EVOLUTION?

While evolutionists claim that natural selection is the best-studied mechanism for evolution, they also must explain the real-life processes behind natural selection. Their discussion of ecology is very interesting (and factual), but it tells us nothing about GTE.

Changing populations within healthy forest ecosystems

For example, PBS 3 devotes a whole segment to show how a healthy forest ecosystem has a large carnivore at the top of the food chain, which can cause drastic changes in the population of the forest. It takes 100 pounds of plant to feed 10 pounds of herbivore, which in turn feed 1 pound of carnivore. So the existence of carnivores indicates the health of the supporting animals and plants. Later on in the program, Wildlife Conservation Society biologist Alan Rabinowitz claims that this healthy forest exhibits "evolution going on around us," but all he means is the replacement of one species with another. Of course, *already-existing* species replacing other already-existing species has nothing to do with the origin of *new* species with new genetic *information*. Once again, "evolution" is a vacuous catch-all term, with any change in population numbers tossed out to the unwary listener as evidence of the goo-to-you theory.

Founder effect

Then the PBS program moves on to isolated habitats and the "founder effect." This is where a single breeding pair or pregnant female colonizes a new niche, and carries only a fraction of the gene pool. Therefore its descendants also contain a small fraction of the original gene pool, so the new population can be very different from the old. This also offers no comfort or support to the notion of evolution because the new population has less information than the old.

Invasion — the leafy spurge

Another ecological topic is biological invaders, the bane of all countries that depend on agriculture and livestock to feed their people and earn export dollars. The invaders are often more mobile and adaptive, so they out-compete native species. Modern technology has vastly increased the rate of hostile invasions, as animals stow away on ships and in the undercarriage of airplanes, although some species have been introduced deliberately. Fordham University paleoecologist David Burney investigated what happened in Hawaii when Polynesians and then Europeans introduced new species. He claimed:

> Evolution has now entered a new mode. Something altogether new is happening, and it has to do with what humans do to the evolutionary process. [PBS 3]

Ho hum, this is just another example of replacement of one species with another, which again has nothing to do with showing how particles could have turned into people.

Pioneers introduced a weed called leafy spurge into North Dakota from Russia, and it "threatens to kill off all native grasses." A cattle rancher claimed on PBS that "it is a cancer to the land . . . it makes the land just totally useless." Actually, the first claim is an exaggeration, and the second is a matter of perspective — sheep and goat farmers would have no problems.

But the rancher said that herbicides were very expensive, so the narrator asks:

> . . . what's left? . . . The solution may be another invader — discovered when scientists learned what kept leafy spurge in check in its native Russia. It's the flea beetle — a case of fighting evolutionary fire with fire. [PBS 3]

Canisters of flea beetles are dropped from airplanes, then the narrator says:

> So now we're in a race most of us don't even know we're running — to learn as much as possible about evolution before it's too late. [PBS 3]

Huh? Using already-existing enemies of the leafy spurge requires "evolution"? This must be the nadir of the contentless nature of this word, even by the pathetic standards of the PBS series. Farmers have used such common-sense biological controls for centuries, well before Darwin. Interestingly, one of the classic cases of successful biological control was the defeat of Australia's cactus invader, the prickly pear, through the introduction of the *Cactoblastis* organism. John Mann, the scientist responsible for saving Australia from ecological and economic ruin in this way, was heaped with accolades and honors for his feat. Mann was a convinced biblical creationist, who was interviewed by *Creation* magazine before his death.[12]

---

12. Interview with creationist biological control expert, Dr. John Mann, M.B.E., *Creation* 5(2):20–21, October 1982.

Symbiosis

PBS 3 also describes the leaf-cutting ants of Brazil. They form colonies containing eight million insects, and they cut leaves into pieces and bring them to the nest, but they don't eat them. Rather, other leafcutter ants mulch them and use the mulch to grow a fungus "garden." This fungus is used as food for the young leafcutters, which thus depend on the fungus for survival, but the fungus depends on the ants to provide the mulch.

But this fungus garden has a "weed," a virulent mold that badly hinders the fungal growth. To combat this, some ants have a white waxy coating that is now known to be tangled mats of bacteria that produce antibiotics that kill the mold.

Presumably, by this stage in the series, the producers hope that viewers are so indoctrinated in evolution that they don't even need to try to produce evidence. To the diehard evolutionist, any phenomenon at all can be adduced as "evidence" for evolution. In this case, they don't bother to explain how such a complex symbiosis could have evolved, but merely assert that the bacteria and mold are products of an arms race lasting 50 million years.

PREDATOR–PREY, DRIVING FORCE OF EVOLUTION?

While evolutionists discuss natural selection and speciation, they like to emphasize the bloodshed and violence that drives these biological changes. They see "Nature, red in tooth and claw," in the memorable phrase from the very long 1850 poem *In Memoriam, A.H.H.* by Alfred Lord Tennyson (1809–1892). In debates they love to pull out this as "knock-down" evidence against Christians, believing it disproves the possibility of a benevolent, wise Creator — following Darwin. The fact that Tennyson's poem predated Darwin's *Origin* indicates that

Darwin was greatly influenced by philosophical ideas of his day.

But their viewpoint overlooks an obvious incident in biblical history — Adam's sin and God's subsequent curse on the whole creation, as I will explain further on. Unfortunately, many in the "intelligent design movement" refuse to invoke the Bible, which provides the *only* plausible answer, so they are stumped by this argument.[13] So, upon closer inspection, the predator–prey paradigm testifies to the accuracy of the biblical account and offers nothing to resolve the fundamental flaw of the general theory of evolution: where does new genetic information come from?

Episode 4 of the PBS *Evolution* series aims to show that these violent biological forces, rather than the environmental ones, drive evolution most strongly, based largely on extensive interviews with the atheistic sociobiologist Edward O. Wilson. The title of PBS 4, "The Evolutionary Arms Race!" reflects the struggle between predator and prey: as a prey evolves stronger defense mechanisms, an attacker must evolve stronger mechanisms to survive, and vice versa. Of course, evolutionary biologists think there is no design behind this: the only prey that survive have *chance* copying mistakes in their genes that confer a strong defense, and they pass on these genes to their offspring. Faced with these stronger defense mechanisms, only those predators that *happen* to have mutations conferring better attacking power will be able to eat the prey, while the others starve and fail to pass on their genes.

But as explained earlier, real evolution requires changes that *increase genetic information*, while non-information-increasing changes are part of the creation model. None of the examples presented in episode 4

13. See Carl Wieland, AiG's views on the intelligent design movement, www.answersingenesis.org/IDM, August 30, 2002.

prove that information has increased, so they provide no support for evolution or against creation.

Poison newt

PBS takes viewers to Oregon, where there were mysterious deaths of campers, but it turned out that newts were found boiled in the coffee pot. These rough-skinned newts (*Taricha granulosa*) secrete a deadly toxin from their skin glands so powerful that even a pinhead-sized amount can kill an adult human. They are the deadliest salamanders on earth. So scientists investigated why this newt should have such a deadly toxin.

They theorized that a predator was driving this "evolution," and they found that the common garter snake (*Thamnophis sirtalis*) was the newt's only predator. Most snakes will be killed by the newt's toxin, but the common garter snake just loses muscle control for a few hours, which could of course have serious consequences. But the newts were also driving the "evolution" of the snakes — they also had various degrees of resistance to the newt toxin.

Are these conclusions correct? Yes, it is probably correct that the predators and prey are driving each other's changes, and that they are the result of mutations and natural selection. Although it might surprise the ill-informed anti-creationist that creationists accept mutations and selection, it shouldn't be so surprising to anyone who understands the biblical creation/Fall model (see chapter 4).

So is this proof of particles-to-people evolution? Not at all. There is no proof that the changes increase genetic information. In fact, the reverse seems to be true.

The snakes with greater resistance have a cost — they move more slowly. Since PBS provided no explanation of the poison's activity, it's fair to propose possible scenarios to explain the phenomenon under a biblical framework (it would be hypocritical for evolutionists to object, since they often produce hypothetical "just-so" stories to explain what they cannot see).

Suppose the newt's poison normally reacts with a particular neurotransmitter in its victims to produce something that halts all nerve impulses, resulting in death. But if the snake had a mutation which *reduced* the production of this neurotransmitter, then the newt's poison would have fewer targets to act upon. Another possibility is a mutation in the snake altering the neurotransmitter's precise structure so that its shape no longer matches the protein. Either way, the poison would be less effective. But at the same time, either mutation would slow nerve impulses, making the snake's muscle movement slower.

So either of these would be an information *loss* in the snake that happens to confer an advantage. This is far from the only example. The best known is sickle-cell anemia, a common blood disorder in which a mutation causes the sufferer's hemoglobin to form the wrong shape and fail to carry oxygen. People who carry two copies of the sickle-cell gene (homozygous) often develop fatal anemia. But this misshapen hemoglobin also resists the malaria parasite (*Plasmodium*). So humans who are heterozygous (have both a normal and abnormal gene) have some advantage in areas where malaria is prevalent, even though half their hemoglobin is less effective at its job of carrying oxygen. Another example is wingless beetles, which survive on windy islands because they won't fly and be blown into the sea.[14]

---

14. See C. Wieland, "Beetle Bloopers. Even a Defect Can Be an Advantage Sometimes," *Creation* 19(3):30 (June–August 1997).

As for the newt, likewise, increased secretion of poison can result without any new information. One possibility is an information-*losing* mutation that disables a gene controlling the production of the poison. Then it would be over-produced, which would be an advantage in defending against the snake, but a wasteful use of resources otherwise.

There are other related examples, e.g., one way that the *Staphylococcus* bacteria becomes resistant to penicillin is via a mutation that disables a control gene for production of penicillinase, an enzyme that destroys penicillin. When it has this mutation, the bacterium *over*-produces this enzyme, which means it is resistant to huge amounts of penicillin. But in the wild, this mutant bacterium is less fit, because it squanders resources by producing unnecessary penicillinase.

Another example is a cattle breed called the *Belgian Blue*. This is very valuable to beef farmers because it has 20–30% more muscle than average cattle, and its meat is lower in fat and very tender. Normally, muscle growth is regulated by a number of proteins, such as *myostatin*. However, Belgian Blues have a mutation that *deactivates* the myostatin gene, so the muscles grow uncontrolled and become very large. This mutation has a cost, in reduced fertility.[15] A different mutation of the same gene is also responsible for the very muscular Piedmontese cattle. Genetic engineers have bred muscular mice by the same principle.

In all these cases, a mutation causes information *loss,* even though it might be considered "beneficial." Therefore it is in the *opposite* direction required for particles-to-people evolution, which requires the generation of *new* information.

15. J. Travis, "Muscle-bound Cattle Reveal Meaty Mutation," *Science News* 152(21):325 (November 22, 1997).

Did God create carnivory?

According to the Bible, the original diet of both humans and animals was vegetarian (Gen. 1:29–30). So how do creationists explain today's carnivory? Episode 4 of the PBS *Evolution* series showed many examples of animals killing other animals, which doesn't seem like a "very good" creation (Gen. 1:31). According to the Bible, death was introduced with Adam's sin (Gen. 2:17; Gen. 3:17–19; Rom. 5:12; 1 Cor. 15:21–22). While these verses refer explicitly to human death, Genesis 3 is clear that Adam's sin had further unpleasant effects because Adam was the federal head of creation. The reformer John Calvin commented on Genesis 3:19:

> Therefore, we may know, that whatever unwholesome things may be produced, are not natural fruits of the earth, but are corruptions which originate from sin.[16]

This is supported by Paul's teaching of Romans 8:20–22, that God subjected the whole creation to futility, and many commentators believe Paul was alluding to Genesis 3. Further support comes from the fact that the restored creation will have no carnivory (Isa. 65:25).

The Bible doesn't specifically explain how carnivory originated, but since creation was finished after day 6 (Gen. 2:1–3), there is no possibility that God created new carnivorous animals. Instead, creationists have three explanations in general, although the specific explanation depends on the particular case.[17]

1. The Bible appears not to regard insects as living in the same sense as humans and vertebrate

---

16. J. Calvin, *Genesis,* 1554 (Edinburgh, UK: Banner of Truth, 1984), p. 180.
17. This topic is covered more fully in chapter 6 of Ken Ham, Andrew Snelling, and Carl Wieland, *The Answers Book* (Green Forest, AR: Master Books, 1990).

animals — the Hebrew never refers to them as *nephesh chayyah* ("living soul/creature"), unlike humans and even fish (Gen. 1:20, 2:7).

2. Before the Fall, many attack/defense structures could have been used in a vegetarian lifestyle. For example, even today, some baby spiders use their webs to trap pollen for food,[18] and there was the case of a lion that wouldn't eat meat.[19] Many poisons actually have beneficial purposes in small amounts.[20] Even PBS pointed out that microbes "help prime the immune system" and that many allergies might be due to a society that's too clean.

3. God foreknew the Fall, so He programmed creatures with the information for design features for attack and defense that they would need in a cursed world. This information was "switched on" at the Fall.

For the poisonous newt, it seems that #3 is the best explanation for the molecular structure of the deadly toxin itself and the poison glands on the skin. In general, I believe #3 is the best explanation for structures that seem specifically designed for attack and defense.

EVOLUTION OF PATHOGENS

If evolutionists hope to find evidence of modern-day evolution, they have a perfect opportunity with pathogens. In just a few months, bacteria can go through hundreds of thousands of generations, equivalent to

18. See "Pollen-Eating Spiders," *Creation* 22(3):8 (June–August 2000); *Nature Australia* (Summer 1999–2000): p. 5.
19. D. Catchpoole, "The Lion That Wouldn't Eat Meat," *Creation* 22(2):22–23 (March–May 2000).
20. See J. Bergman, "Understanding Poisons from a Creationist Perspective," *TJ* 11(3):353–360, 1997; <www.answersingenesis.org/poison>.

"millions of years" in vertebrates. Yet in spite of this rapid change, the bacteria that we see today are essentially the same as the bacteria retrieved from the tombs of the pharaohs, and even with those discovered in salt crystals "dated" millions of years old.[21]

HIV resistance to drugs

PBS 1 claims that Darwin didn't really see evolution in action, but now we do. Supposedly HIV, the cause of AIDS, evolves resistance to drugs faster than we can make them. Because the virus can produce billions of copies per day, it can "evolve" in minutes to hours. One researcher said that this rapid change would be a "surprise" if we didn't have the concept of evolution. PBS also attempted to tug heartstrings, by portraying AIDS patients as "victims of evolution."

First, we see the equivocation — HIV producing HIV is supposed to show that particles could turn into people; but they're still HIV — they haven't changed into something else.

Second, in PBS 4, it's made clear that the related phenomenon of antibiotic resistance in bacteria took the medical community by surprise — this means that it wasn't a prediction of evolution, except after the fact.

Third, they fail to demonstrate that new information is involved, and in fact the next segment of the program showed that the opposite is true. Veronica Miller of Goethe University in Germany experimented by ceasing all antiviral drug treatments to a patient. Without the drugs, the few surviving original ("wild") types that had infected the patient could grow more easily. It turned out that they easily out-competed the vast numbers of resistant forms that had developed in the hospital. She said this was a risk because the wild types were also more

21. D. Batten, *Creation* 24(4):10–13 (September–November 2002).

dangerous — more efficient than the new strains that had survived the earlier drug treatments. The superior efficiency and reproductive success of the wild type implies that the other "evolved" strains acquired resistance due to a *loss* of information somewhere.

This should not be surprising, because the same is true of many examples of antibiotic resistance in bacteria. For example, some bacteria (see pages 90 through 93) have an enzyme that usually has a useful purpose, but it also turns an antibiotic into a poison. That is, it's not the antibiotic *per se* that's damaging, but its chemical byproduct from the bacterium's metabolism. So a mutation *disabling* this enzyme would render the antibiotic harmless. But this bacterium is still disabled, because the enzyme is now hindered, so the bacterium would be unable to compete in the wild with non-resistant ones. The information loss in both HIV and the bacterium is the *opposite* of what evolution requires.[22]

Tuberculosis and antibiotic resistance

PBS describes the microbe as a "predator" of humans, although "parasite" would be more accurate. Mummies show that the tuberculosis bacillus (TB) affected Egyptians 4,000 years ago. The Black Death wiped out one-third of Europe's population in 1347–1351, and the influenza pandemic of 1918–1919 killed 20 million people — more than World War 1 that had just ended.

After the world wars, antibiotics were considered the "magic bullet," and there were optimistic claims even as late as 1969 that "infectious diseases were a thing of the past." But they failed to anticipate the development of resistance. This shows that bacterial resistance was hardly

---

22. For more information on bacterial and viral resistance to drugs see C. Wieland, "Superbugs: Not Super After All," *Creation* 20(1):10–13 (Dec. 1997–Feb. 1998); "Has AIDS Evolved?" *Creation* 12(3):29–32 (June–August 1990); J. Sarfati, "Anthrax and Antibiotics: Is Evolution Relevant?" <http://www.answersingenesis.org/anthrax>.

a "prediction" of evolution, but is really a phenomenon they try to explain "after the fact" as due to evolution. As will be shown, there is nothing to support molecules-to-man evolution; rather, a properly understood creation model makes good sense of the evidence.

PBS 4 discussed a new strain of TB that had arisen in the overcrowded Russian prison system, containing malnourished prisoners with weakened immune systems. One inmate, "Sasha" (Alexandr), had failed to complete his course of antibiotics. This meant that a few bacteria survived because they had some resistance to the antibiotic, and then proliferated once the treatment stopped. But the program itself makes it clear that the resistance was already present, so this is *not* evolution, although it *is* natural selection.

These resistant bacteria are not confined to the prison, but have spread because of travel. One 19-year-old Russian student, "Anna," has a strain resistant to five antibiotics. Immunologists predict that TB could soon claim 2–3 million lives per year.

But as shown, there is no proof that any antibiotic resistance is due to increased genetic information. The above example shows that the information was *already present*, and I previously explained how a *loss* of information could confer resistance. Sometimes bacteria can pass genes to each other by exchanging plasmids, and sometimes these genes confer resistance. But of course, these examples involve no new information produced in the biosphere.

Evolution of less harmful bacteria?

Paul Ewald of Amherst College claimed on PBS 4 that "evolution" may not only be a problem, but could also be harnessed to "evolve" less harmful bacteria. If a pathogen spreads by close contact between people, then it's in its best interest not to make people so sick that they can't move around. But those pathogens spread by water and insects tend to be deadly.

In the 1991 cholera epidemic in South America, a million people were infected, and 10,000 died. The bacterium (*Vibrio cholerae*) was spread by contaminated water, so "evolved" high levels of toxicity. The solution was to clean the water supply, so that only healthier people could spread the germ. So the germ "evolved" mildness, and many infected people didn't even develop symptoms.

But here again, there is indeed natural selection, but the result is that *Vibrio cholerae* turn into *Vibrio cholerae!* There is no proof that any new information was produced, but rather, selection of existing genetic variation.

PBS 4 compared this phenomenon to breeding domestic dogs from wolves, but again this involved *loss* of information.

Pathogens and creation

Some people wonder where disease germs fit into the biblical framework, if God created everything "very good." Under this framework, obviously the Fall was responsible for disease, but how, if God had finished creating at the end of creation week? The phenomenon described in the previous section can provide some insights. It clearly shows that even something usually known as a deadly germ can have a mild variant that causes no illness. Presumably something like this was created during creation week — even today, *Vibrio cholerae* has a role in the ecosystems of brackish waters and estuaries, and the original may have had a role living symbiotically with some people. Even its toxin probably has a beneficial function in small amounts, like most poisons. The virulence arose after the Fall, by natural selection of varieties producing more and more toxin as contaminated water became more plentiful. No new information would be needed for this process. Recent evidence shows that the *loss* of *chemotaxis* — the ability to move in response to changes in chemical concentrations — will markedly increase infectivity in an infant mouse model of cholera.[23]

Another likely example of virulence arising by information loss is the mycoplasmas, the smallest known self-reproducing organisms (parasitic bacteria with no cell walls and fewer than 1,000 genes, found in the respiratory system and urogenital tracts of humans). Loss of genetic information, e.g., for amino acid synthesis, could have resulted in the mycoplasmas becoming increasingly dependent on their hosts for survival.[24] Some clues to possible benign pre-Fall roles for viruses can be gleaned from functions they have even today. Viruses are non-living entities, which function like seeds and spores, transporting genes among plants and animals. They also help keep soil fertile, keep water clean, and regulate gases in the atmosphere.[25] So once again, some alleged evidence for evolution actually provides support for the creation/Fall model.

Has immunity evolved?

In PBS 4, Stephen O'Brien of the National Cancer Institute wondered why the big cats have "evolved" resistance to a disease deadly to humans. There is a Feline Immunodeficiency Virus (FIV) that should cause AIDS-like symptoms. Supposedly the cats' ancestors were almost

23. D.S. Merrell et al., "Host-induced Epidemic Spread of the Cholera Bacterium," *Nature* 417(6889):642–644 (June 6, 2002).
24. T.C. Wood, "Genome Decay in the Mycoplasmas," *Impact* 340 (October 2001); <www.icr.org/pubs/imp/imp-340.htm>; C. Wieland, "Diseases on the Ark" (Answering the Critics), *TJ* 8(1):16–18, 1994, explains important related concepts.
25. J. Bergman, "Did God Make Pathogenic Viruses?" *TJ* 13(1):115–125, 1999.

wiped out by the virus, but some had resistant genes. Supposedly, the FIV evolved to mildness.

More interesting was the claim that about 10 percent of humans have a "whopping mutation" that confers resistance to HIV. This turns out to be the *loss* of certain receptors on the immune cells preventing the HIV from docking on them. Again, this change is in the *opposite direction* required to change particles into people.

From mycoplasmas to big cats, from TB to poison newts, there's not a shred of evidence that might explain the evolution of new genetic information, but the *loss* that we see fits nicely with the biblical creationist model.

CHAPTER 5

ARGUMENT: SOME MUTATIONS ARE BENEFICIAL

Evolutionists say, "Mutations and other
biological mechanisms have been observed to
produce new features in organisms."

W hen they begin to talk about mutations, evolutionists tacitly acknowledge that natural
selection, by itself, cannot explain the rise of
new genetic information. Somehow they have to explain
the introduction of completely new genetic instructions
for feathers and other wonders that never existed in "simpler" life forms. So they place their faith in mutations.

In the process of defending mutations as a mechanism for creating new genetic code, they attack a straw-
man version of the creationist model, and they have *no*
answer for the creationists' real scientific objections. *Scientific American* states this common straw-man position
and their answer to it.

10. MUTATIONS ARE ESSENTIAL TO EVOLUTION
THEORY, BUT MUTATIONS CAN ONLY ELIMINATE
TRAITS. THEY CANNOT PRODUCE NEW
FEATURES.

> On the contrary, biology has catalogued many traits produced by point mutations (changes at precise positions in an organism's DNA) — bacterial resistance to antibiotics, for example. [*SA* 82]

This is a serious misstatement of the creationist argument. The issue is not *new traits*, but new genetic *information*. In no known case is antibiotic resistance the result of new information. There are several ways that an information *loss* can confer resistance, as already discussed. We have also pointed out in various ways how new traits, even helpful, adaptive traits, can arise through *loss* of genetic information (which is to be expected from mutations).

> Mutations that arise in the homeobox (*Hox*) family of development-regulating genes in animals can also have complex effects. *Hox* genes direct where legs, wings, antennae, and body segments should grow. In fruit flies, for instance, the mutation called *Antennapedia* causes legs to sprout where antennae should grow. [*SA* 82]

Once again, there is no new information! Rather, a mutation in the hox gene (see next section) results in already-existing information being switched on in the wrong place.[1] The hox gene merely moved legs to the wrong place; it did not produce any of the information that actually constructs the legs, which in ants and bees include a wondrously complex mechanical and hydraulic mechanism that enables these insects to stick to surfaces.[2]

---

1. See D. Batten, "Hox (homeobox) Genes — Evolution's Saviour?" <www.answersingenesis.org/docs/4205.asp> and D. DeWitt, "Hox Hype — Has Macro-evolution Been Proven?" <www.answersingenesis.org/docs2002/0215hox_hype.asp>.
2. See J. Sarfati, "Startling Stickiness," *Creation* 24(2):37 (March–May 2002).

These abnormal limbs are not functional, but their existence demonstrates that genetic mistakes can produce complex structures, which natural selection can then test for possible uses. [*SA* 82]

Amazing — natural selection can "test for possible uses" of "non-functional" (i.e., *useless!*) limbs in the wrong place. Such deformities would be active hindrances to survival.

GENE SWITCHES: MEANS OF EVOLUTION?

William Bateson (1861–1926), who added the word "genetics" to our vocabulary in 1909, found that embryos sometimes grew body parts in the wrong place. From this he theorized that there are underlying controls of certain body parts, and other controls governing where they go.

Ed Lewis investigated and won a Nobel Prize in 1995 for discovering a small set of genes that affect different body parts (*Hox* or *Homeobox*). They act like "architects of the body." Mutations in these can cause "dramatic" changes. Many experiments have been performed on fruit flies (*Drosophila*), where poisons and radiation induced mutations.

The problem is that they are always harmful. PBS 2 showed an extra pair of wings on a fly, but failed to mention that they were a *hindrance* to flying because there are no accompanying muscles. Both these flies would be *eliminated* by natural selection.

Walter Gehring of the University of Basel (Switzerland) replaced a gene needed for eye development in a fruit fly with the corresponding gene from a mouse. The fly still developed normal fly eyes, i.e., compound eyes rather than lens/camera. This gene in both insects and mammals is called *eyeless* because absence of this gene means no eyes will form.

However, there is obviously more to the differences between different animals. Eyeless is a *switch* — it turns on the genetic information needed for eyes. But evolution requires some way of generating the new information that's to be switched on. The information needed to build a compound eye is vastly different from that needed to build a lens/camera type of eye. By analogy, the *same* switch on an electric outlet/power socket can turn on a light or a laptop, but this hardly proves that a light evolved into a laptop!

All the same, the program says that *eyeless* is one of a small number of common genes used in the embryonic development of many animals. The program illustrated this with diagrams. Supposedly, all evolution needed to do was reshuffle packets of information into different combinations.

But as shown, known mutations in these genes cause monstrosities, and different switches are very distinct from what is switched on or off. Also, the embryo develops into its basic body plan *before* these genes start switching — obviously they can't be the cause of the plan before they are activated! But the common genes make perfect sense given the existence of a *single* Creator.

INCREASED *AMOUNTS* OF DNA DON'T MEAN INCREASED *FUNCTION*

Biologists have discovered a whole range of mechanisms that can cause radical changes in the amount of DNA possessed by an organism. Gene duplication, polyploidy, insertions, etc., do not help explain evolution, however. They represent an increase in *amount* of DNA, but not an increase in the amount of functional genetic *information* — these mechanisms create nothing new.

Macroevolution needs *new* genes (for making feathers on reptiles, for example), yet *Scientific American* completely misses this simple distinction:

> Moreover, molecular biology has discovered mechanisms for genetic change that go beyond point mutations, and these expand the ways in which new traits can appear. Functional modules within genes can be spliced together in novel ways. Whole genes can be accidentally duplicated in an organism's DNA, and the duplicates are free to mutate into genes for new, complex features. [*SA* 82]

In plants, but not in animals (possibly with rare exceptions), the doubling of all the chromosomes may result in an individual which can no longer interbreed with the parent type — this is called *polyploidy*. Although this may technically be called a new species, because of the reproductive isolation, no new information has been produced, just repetitious doubling of *existing* information. If a malfunction in a printing press caused a book to be printed with every page doubled, it would not be more informative than the proper book. (Brave students of evolutionary professors might like to ask whether they would get extra marks for handing in two copies of the same assignment.)

Duplication of a single chromosome is normally harmful, as in Down's syndrome. Insertions are a very efficient way of completely destroying the functionality of existing genes. Biophysicist Dr. Lee Spetner in his book *Not By Chance* analyzes examples of mutational changes that evolutionists have claimed to have been increases in information, and shows that they are actually examples of *loss of specificity*, which means they involved loss of information (which is to be expected from information theory).

The evolutionist's "gene duplication idea" is that an existing gene may be doubled, and one copy does its normal work while the other copy is redundant and non-expressed. Therefore, it is free to mutate free of selection pressure (to get rid of it). However, such "neutral" mutations are powerless to produce new genuine information. Dawkins and others point out that natural selection is the only possible naturalistic explanation for the immense design in nature (not a good one, as Spetner and others have shown). Dawkins and others propose that random changes produce a new function, then this redundant gene becomes expressed somehow and is fine-tuned under the natural selective process.

This "idea" is just a lot of hand-waving. It relies on a chance copying event, genes somehow being switched off, randomly mutating to something approximating a new function, then being switched on again so natural selection can tune it.

Furthermore, mutations do not occur in just the duplicated gene; they occur throughout the genome. Consequently, all the deleterious mutations in the rest of the genome have to be eliminated by the death of the unfit. Selective mutations in the target duplicate gene are extremely rare — it might represent only 1 part in 30,000 of the genome of an animal. The larger the genome, the bigger the problem, because the larger the genome, the lower the mutation rate that the creature can sustain without error catastrophe; as a result, it takes even longer for *any* mutation to occur, let alone a desirable one, in the duplicated gene. There just has not been enough time for such a naturalistic process to account for the amount of genetic information that we see in living things.

Dawkins and others have recognized that the "information space" possible within just one gene is so huge that random changes without some guiding force could never come up with a new function. There could never be enough "experiments" (mutating generations of organisms) to find anything useful by such a process. Note that an average gene of 1,000 base pairs represents 4^{1000} possibilities — that is 10^{602} (compare this with the number of atoms in the universe estimated at "only" 10^{80}). If every atom in the universe represented an "experiment" every millisecond for the supposed 15 billion years of the universe, this could only try a maximum 10^{100} of the possibilities for the gene. So such a "neutral" process cannot possibly find any sequence with specificity (usefulness), even allowing for the fact that more than just one sequence may be functional to some extent.

So Dawkins and company have the same problem as the advocates of neutral selection theory. Increasing knowledge of the molecular basis of biological functions has exploded the known "information space" so that mutations and natural selection — with or without gene duplication, or any other known natural process — cannot account for the irreducibly complex nature of living systems.

Yet *Scientific American* has the impertinence to claim:

> Comparisons of the DNA from a wide variety of organisms indicate that this [duplication of genes] is how the globin family of blood proteins evolved over millions of years. [*SA* 82]

This is about the vital red blood pigment *hemoglobin* that carries the oxygen. It has four polypeptide chains and iron. Evolutionists believe that this evolved from an oxygen-carrying iron-containing protein called *myoglobin* found in muscles, which has only one polypeptide chain. However, there is no *demonstration* that gene duplication

plus natural selection turned the one-chained myoglobin into the four-chained hemoglobin. Nor is there any
adequate explanation of how the hypothetical intermediates would have had selective advantages.

In fact, the proposed evolution of hemoglobin is far
more complicated than *Scientific American* implies,
though it requires a little advanced biology to understand. The α- and β-globin chains are encoded on genes
on different chromosomes, so they are expressed independently. This expression must be controlled precisely,
otherwise various types of anemia called *thalassemia*
result. Also, there is an essential protein called AHSP
(alpha hemoglobin stabilizing protein) which, as the
name implies, stabilizes the α-chain, and also brings it
to the β-chain. Otherwise the α-chain would precipitate
and damage the red blood cells.

AHSP is one of many examples of a class of protein
called *chaperones* which govern the folding of other proteins.[4] This is yet another problem for chemical evolutionary theories — how did the first proteins fold correctly without chaperones? And since chaperones themselves are complex proteins, how did *they* fold?[5]

Identifying information-increasing mutations may be
a small part of the whole evolutionary discussion, but it
is a critical "weak link" in the logical chain. PBS, *Scientific American,* and every other pro-evolution propaganda machine have failed to identify any evidence that
might strengthen this straw link.

---

4. A. Kihm et al., "An Abundant Erythroid Protein That Stabilizes Free-
   haemoglobin," *Nature* 417(6890):758–763 (June 13, 2002); comment by L.
   Luzzatto and R. Notaro, "Haemoglobin's Chaperone," same issue, p. 703–705.
5. See S.E. Aw, "The Origin of Life: A Critique of Current Scientific Models," *TJ*
   10(3):300–314, 1996.

CHAPTER 6

ARGUMENT: COMMON DESIGN POINTS TO COMMON ANCESTRY

Evolutionists say, "Studies have found amazing similarities in DNA and biological systems — solid evidence that life on earth has a common ancestor."

COMMON STRUCTURES = COMMON ANCESTRY?

In most arguments for evolution, the debater assumes that common physical features, such as five fingers on apes and humans, point to a common ancestor in the distant past. Darwin mocked the idea (proposed by Richard Owen on the PBS dramatization of his encounter with Darwin) that common structures (homologies) were due to a common creator rather than a common ancestor.

But the common Designer explanation makes much more sense of the findings of modern geneticists, who have discovered just how *different* the genetic blueprint can be behind many apparent similarities in the anatomical structures that Darwin saw. *Genes* are inherited, not structures *per se*. So one would expect the similarities, if they were the result of evolutionary common ancestry, to be produced by a common genetic program (this may or may not be the case for common design). But in many cases, this is clearly not so. Consider the example of the five digits of both frogs and humans — the human embryo develops a ridge at the limb tip, then material between the digits dissolves; in frogs, the digits grow outward from buds (see diagram below). This argues strongly against the "common ancestry" evolutionary explanation for the similarity.

The PBS program and other evolutionary propagandists claim that the DNA code is universal, and proof of a common ancestor. But this is false — there are exceptions, some known since the 1970s, not only in mitochondrial but also nuclear DNA sequencing. An example

Development of Human and Frog Digits

Human   **Frog**

Stylized diagram showing the difference in developmental patterns of frog and human digits.
Left: In humans, programmed cell death (*apoptosis*) divides the ridge into five regions that then develop into digits (fingers and toes).
[From T.W. Sadler, editor, *Langman's Medical Embryology*, 7th ed. (Baltimore, MD: Williams and Wilkins, 1995), p. 154–157.]
Right: In frogs, the digits grow outward from buds as cells divide.
[From M.J. Tyler, *Australian Frogs: A Natural History* (Sydney, Australia: Reed New Holland, 1999), p. 80.]

is *Paramecium*, where a few of the 64 codons code for different amino acids. More examples are being found constantly.[1] The Discovery Institute has pointed out this clear factual error in the PBS program.[2] Also, some organisms code for one or two extra amino acids beyond the main 20 types.[3]

The reaction by the PBS spokeswoman, Eugenie Scott, showed how the evolutionary establishment is more concerned with promoting evolution than scientific accuracy. Instead of conceding that the PBS show was wrong, she attacked the messengers, citing statements calling their (correct!) claim "so bizarre as to be almost beyond belief." Then she even implicitly conceded the truth of the claim by citing this explanation: "Those exceptions, however, are known to have derived from organisms that had the standard code."

To paraphrase: "It was wrong to point out that there really are exceptions, even though it's true; and it was right for the PBS to imply something that wasn't true because we can explain why it's not always true."

But assuming the truth of Darwinism as "evidence" for their explanation is begging the question. There is no experimental evidence, since we lack the DNA code of these alleged ancestors. There is also the theoretical problem that if we change the code, then the wrong proteins would be made, and the organism would die — so once a code is settled on, we're stuck with it. The Discovery Institute also demonstrated the illogic of Scott's

---

1. National Institutes of Health <www.ncbi.nlm.nih.gov/htbin-post/Taxonomy/wprintgc?mode=c>, August 29, 2002.
2. September 10, 2001 press release, "PBS Charged with 'False Claim' on 'Universal Genetic Code,' " <www.reviewevolution.com/press/pressRelease_FalseClaim.php>.
3. Certain archaea and eubacteria code for 21st or 22nd amino acids, selenocysteine and pyrrolysine — see J.F. Atkins and R. Gesteland, "The 22nd Amino Acid," *Science* 296(5572):1409–10, May 24, 2002; commentary on technical papers on p. 1459–62 and 1462–66.

claim.[4] Certainly most of the code is universal, but this is best explained by common design. Of all the millions of genetic codes possible, ours, or something almost like it, is optimal for protecting against errors.[5] But the exceptions thwart evolutionary explanations.

DNA COMPARISONS — SUBJECT TO INTERPRETATION

Scientific American repeats the common argument that DNA comparisons help scientists to reconstruct the evolutionary development of organisms:

> Macroevolution studies how taxonomic groups above the level of species change. Its evidence draws frequently from the fossil record and DNA comparisons to reconstruct how various organisms may be related. [*SA* 80]

DNA comparisons are just a subset of the *homology* argument, which makes just as much sense in a biblical framework. A *common Designer* is another interpretation that makes sense of the *same* data. An architect commonly uses the same building material for different buildings, and a car maker commonly uses the same parts in different cars. So we shouldn't be surprised if a Designer for life used the same biochemistry and structures in many different creatures. Conversely, if all living organisms were totally different, this might look like there were *many* designers instead of one.

Since DNA codes for structures and biochemical molecules, we should expect the most similar creatures

---

4. September 20, 2001, press release, "Offscreen, 'Evolution' Spokesperson Tries to Tar Scientific Critics Who Are Ignored," </www.reviewevolution.com/press/pressRelease_ScientistsTar.php>.
5. J. Knight, "Top Translator," *New Scientist* 158(2130):15 (April 18, 1998). Natural selection cannot explain this code optimality, since there is no way to replace the first functional code with a "better" one without destroying functionality.

to have the most similar DNA. Apes and humans are both mammals, with similar shapes, so both have similar DNA. We should expect humans to have more DNA similarities with another mammal like a pig than with a reptile like a rattlesnake. And this is so. Humans are very different from yeast but they have some biochemistry in common, so we should expect human DNA to differ more from yeast DNA than from ape DNA.

So the general pattern of similarities need not be explained by common-ancestry (evolution). Furthermore, there are some puzzling anomalies for an evolutionary explanation — similarities between organisms that evolutionists don't believe are closely related. For example, hemoglobin, the complex molecule that carries oxygen in blood and results in its red color, is found in vertebrates. But it is also found in *some* earthworms, starfish, crustaceans, mollusks, and even in some bacteria. An antigen receptor protein has the same unusual single chain structure in camels and nurse sharks, but this cannot be explained by a common ancestor of sharks and camels.[6] And there are many other examples of similarities that cannot be due to evolution.

DEBUNKING THE "MOLECULAR CLOCK"

Scientific American repeats the common canard that DNA gives us a "molecular clock" that tells us the history of DNA's evolution from the simplest life form to mankind:

> Nevertheless, evolutionists can cite further supportive evidence from molecular biology. All organisms share most of the same genes, but as evolution predicts, the structures of these genes

---

6. "Proceedings of the National Academy of Sciences," 95:11,804; cited in *New Scientist* 160(2154):23 (October 3, 1998).

and their products diverge among species, in keeping with their evolutionary relationships. Geneticists speak of the "molecular clock" that records the passage of time. These molecular data also show how various organisms are transitional within evolution. [*SA* 83]

Actually, the molecular clock has many problems for the evolutionist. Not only are there the anomalies and common Designer arguments I mentioned above, but they actually support a creation of distinct types within ordered groups, not continuous evolution, as non-creationist microbiologist Dr. Michael Denton pointed out in *Evolution: A Theory in Crisis*. For example, when comparing the amino acid sequence of cytochrome C of a bacterium (a prokaryote) with such widely diverse eukaryotes as yeast, wheat, silkmoth, pigeon, and horse, all of these have practically the same percentage difference with the bacterium (64–69%). There is no intermediate cytochrome between prokaryotes and eukaryotes, and no hint that the "higher" organism such as a horse has diverged more than the "lower" organism such as the yeast.

The same sort of pattern is observed when comparing cytochrome C of the invertebrate silkmoth with the vertebrates lamprey, carp, turtle, pigeon, and horse. All the vertebrates are equally divergent from the silkmoth (27–30%). Yet again, comparing globins of a lamprey (a "primitive" cyclostome or jawless fish) with a carp, frog, chicken, kangaroo, and human, they are all about equidistant (73–81%). Cytochrome C's compared between a carp and a bullfrog, turtle, chicken, rabbit, and horse yield a constant difference of 13–14%. There is no trace of any transitional series of cyclostome →fish →amphibian →reptile →mammal or bird.

Another problem for evolutionists is how the molecular clock could have ticked so evenly in any given protein in so many different organisms (despite some anomalies discussed earlier which present even more problems). For this to work, there must be a constant mutation rate per unit *time* over most types of organism. But *observations* show that there is a constant mutation rate per *generation*, so it should be much faster for organisms with a fast generation time, such as bacteria, and much slower for elephants. In insects, generation times range from weeks in flies to many years in cicadas, and yet there is no evidence that flies are more diverged than cicadas. So evidence is *against* the theory that the observed patterns are due to mutations accumulating over time as life evolved.

CHAPTER 7

ARGUMENT: "BAD DESIGN" IS EVIDENCE OF LEFTOVERS FROM EVOLUTION

Evolutionists say, "Nature is filled with
evidence of bad design — obvious leftovers from
our evolutionary past, such as 'junk DNA,'
vestigial organs, and eye imperfections."

THE INVERTED EYE — EXAMPLE OF BAD DESIGN?

Kenneth Miller, the Roman Catholic evolutionist who is featured prominently on PBS 1,
claims that the eye has "profound optical imperfections," so is proof of "tinkering" and "blind" natural selection. Miller hasn't presented an argument *for* evolution *per se* at all — because he presents no step-by-
step way for the retina to have evolved — but it is purely
an attack on a Designer. Which is, of course, also an
attack on Miller's own Darwinian version of "god," one
who has chosen to create indirectly (via evolution).

Miller raised the old canard of the backwardly wired
vertebrate retina, as he has done elsewhere. The narrator

even claimed that the eye's "nerves interfere with images," and that the so-called "blind spot" is a serious problem. But these arguments have been refuted before, as shown below.

It would be nice if anti-creationists actually learned something about the eye before making such claims (Miller is unqualified in both physical optics and eye anatomy), or even showed that the eye didn't function properly as a result. In fact, any engineer who designed something remotely as good as the eye would probably win a Nobel Prize! If Miller and the PBS producers disagree, then I challenge them to design a better eye with all the versatility of the vertebrate eye (color perception, resolution, coping with range of light intensity, night vision as well as day vision, etc.)! And this must be done under the constraints of embryonic development.

The retina can detect a single photon of light, and it's impossible to improve on this sensitivity! More than that, it has a *dynamic range* of 10 billion (10^{10}) to one; that is, it will still work well in an intensity of 10 billion photons. Modern photographic film has a dynamic range of only 1,000 to one. Even specialist equipment hasn't anywhere near the dynamic range of the eye, and I have considerable experience in state-of-the-art supersensitive photomultipliers. My Ph.D. thesis and published papers in secular journals largely involve a technique called *Raman spectroscopy*, which analyzes extremely weak scattering at a slightly different frequency from that of the incident laser radiation. The major equipment hazard for Raman spectroscopists is scanning at the incident frequency — the still weak Rayleigh scattering at the same frequency would blow the photomultiplier (the newer ones have an automatic shut-off). I managed to safely scan the Rayleigh line (for calibration) only by using filters to attenuate the intensity of light entering the photomultiplier by a factor of 10^{-7} to 10^{-8}. But having to take such an extreme safety precaution made me envious and admiring of the way the eye is so brilliantly designed to cope with a far wider range of intensities.

Another amazing design feature of the retina is the signal processing that occurs even before the information is transmitted to the brain, in the retinal layers between the ganglion cells and the photoreceptors. For example, a process called *edge extraction* enhances the recognition of edges of objects. Dr. John Stevens, an associate professor of physiology and biomedical engineering, pointed out that it would take "a minimum of a hundred years of Cray [supercomputer] time to simulate what takes place in your eye many times each second."[1] And the retina's analog computing needs far less power than the digital supercomputers and is elegant in its simplicity. Once again, the eye outstrips any human technology, this time in another area.

Someone who *does* know about eye design is the ophthalmologist Dr. George Marshall, who said:

> The idea that the eye is wired backward comes from a lack of knowledge of eye function and anatomy.

He explained that the nerves could not go behind the eye, because that space is reserved for the choroid, which provides the rich blood supply needed for the very metabolically active retinal pigment epithelium (RPE). This is necessary to regenerate the photoreceptors, and to absorb excess heat. So it is necessary for the nerves to go in front instead. The claim on the program that they interfere with the image is blatantly false, because the

---

1. *Byte*, April 1985.

nerves are virtually transparent because of their small size and also having about the same refractive index as the surrounding vitreous humor. In fact, what limits the eye's resolution is the diffraction of light waves at the pupil (proportional to the wavelength and inversely proportional to the pupil's size), so alleged improvements of the retina would make no difference.

It's important to note that the "superior" design of Miller with the (virtually transparent) nerves behind the photoreceptors would require either:

- The choroid in front of the retina — but the choroid is opaque because of all the red blood cells, so this design would be as useless as an eye with a hemorrhage!

- Photoreceptors not in contact with the RPE and choroid at all — but the photoreceptors would be slow to regenerate, so it would probably take months before we could drive after we were photographed with a flashbulb.

Some evolutionists claim that the cephalopod eye is somehow "right," i.e., with nerves behind the receptor, and the program showed photographs of these creatures (e.g., octopus, squid) during this segment. But no one who has actually bothered to study these eyes could make such claims with integrity. In fact, cephalopods don't see as well as humans, and the octopus eye structure is totally different and much simpler. It's more like "a compound eye with a single lens."

Ophthalmologist Peter Gurney gives a detailed response to the question "Is the inverted retina really 'bad design'?"[2] He addresses the claim that the blind spot is

---

2. P. Gurney, "Is Our 'Inverted' Retina Really 'Bad Design'?" *TJ* 13(1):37–44, 1999.

bad design, by pointing out that the blind spot occupies only 0.25% of the visual field, and is far (15°) from the visual axis so that the visual acuity of the region is only about 15% of the foveola, the most sensitive area of the retina right on the visual axis. So the alleged defect is only theoretical, not practical. The blind spot is not considered handicap enough to stop a one-eyed person from driving a private motor vehicle. The main problem with only one eye is the lack of stereoscopic vision.

The program also alleges that the retina is badly designed because it can detach and cause blindness. But this doesn't happen with the vast majority of people, indicating that the design is pretty good. In fact, retinal detachment is more due to the *vitreous* ("glassy") *humor* liquefying from its normally fairly rigid gel state with advancing age. Then the remaining gel pulls away from the retina, leaving tiny holes, so the other liquefied humor can lift off the retina. So one recently devised treatment is draining the liquid and injecting magnetized silicone gel, which can be moved into place with a magnetic field, to push the retina back and block the holes.[3] The occasional failures in the eye with increasing age reflect the fact that we live in a fallen world — so what we observe today may have deteriorated from the original physically perfect state, where, for example, deterioration with age didn't occur.

To answer other alleged "bad design" arguments, there are two principles to consider:

1. Do we have all the information/knowledge on the issue?
2. Could this particular biological system have gone downhill since the Fall?

Related evolutionary arguments are used to attack so-called vestigial organs (see appendix), the panda's thumb, and so-called "junk" DNA.

PANDA'S "THUMB"

Evolutionists have long cited the panda's clumsy-looking "thumb" as evidence of evolution, rather than intelligent design. Gould even wrote a book called *The Panda's Thumb: More Reflections in Natural History* (1980) which says that the panda's thumb "wins no prize in an engineer's derby."[4]

On closer inspection, however, there is nothing clumsy at all about the panda's design.[5] Instead, the "thumb" is part of an elaborate and efficient grasping structure that enables the panda to strip leaves from bamboo shoots.[6]

Claims that the panda's thumb is some kind of nondesigned "contraption" is a smokescreen to distract from the real question — that evolution simply does not explain how life could start in a pond and finish with a panda.

"JUNK" DNA

Each time that evolutionists discover new sections of DNA that have no known function, they like to describe it as "junk" DNA that is a leftover of evolution. For example, the DNA of organisms more complex than bacteria contains regions called *exons* that code for proteins, and non-coding regions called *introns*. So the introns are removed and the exons are "spliced" together to form the mRNA (messenger RNA) that is

---

4. S.J. Gould, *The Panda's Thumb: More Reflections in Natural History* (New York, NY: W.W. Norton & Co., 1980), p. 24.
5. See John Woodmorappe, "The Panda Thumbs Its Nose at the Dysteleological Arguments of the Atheist Stephen Jay Gould," *TJ* 13(1):45–48, 1999.
6. H. Endo et al., "Role of the Giant Panda's 'Pseudo-thumb'," *Nature* 397(6717):309–310, 1999.

finally decoded to form the protein. This also requires elaborate machinery called a *spliceosome*. This assembles on the intron, chops it out at the right place, and joins the exons together. This must be in the right direction and place, because it makes a huge difference if the exon is joined even one letter off.

But it's absurd even on the face of it that more complex organisms should evolve such elaborate machinery to splice the introns if they were really useless. Rather, natural selection would favor organisms that did *not* have to waste resources processing a genome filled with 98 percent of junk. And there have been many uses for junk DNA discovered, such as the overall genome structure and regulation of genes, and to enable rapid post-Flood diversification.[7] Also, damage to introns can be disastrous — one example was deleting four "letters" in the center of an intron, preventing the spliceosome from binding to it, resulting in the intron being included.[8] Mutations in introns interfere with imprinting, the process by which only certain maternal or paternal genes are expressed, not both. Expression of both genes results in a variety of diseases and cancers.[9]

Dr. John Mattick of the University of Queensland in Brisbane, Australia, has published a number of papers arguing that the non-coding DNA regions, or rather their non-coding RNA "negatives," are important for a complicated genetic network.[10] These interact with each

---

7. For an overview, see L. Walkup, "Junk DNA: Evolutionary Discards or God's Tools?" *TJ* 14(2):18–30, 2000.
8. P. Cohen, "New Genetic Spanner in the Works," *New Scientist* 173(2334):17 (March 16, 2002).
9. Don Batten, " 'Junk' DNA (Again)," *TJ* 12(1):5, 1998.
10. J.S. Mattick, "Non-coding RNAs: The Architects of Eukaryotic Complexity," *EMBO Reports* 2:986–991 (November 2001); <http://embo-reports.oupjournals.org/cgi/content/abstract/2/11/986>; M. Cooper, Life 2.0, *New Scientist* 174(2346):30–33 (June 8, 2002); C. Dennis, "The Brave New World of RNA," *Nature* 418(6894):122–124 (July 11, 2002).

other, the DNA, mRNA, and the proteins. Mattick proposes that the introns function as *nodes*, linking points in a network. The introns provide many extra connections, to enable what in computer terminology would be called multi-tasking and parallel processing.

In the case of life, this could control the order in which genes are switched on and off. This means that a tremendous variety of multicellular life could be produced by rewiring the network. In contrast, "early computers were like simple organisms, very cleverly designed, but programmed for one task at a time."[11] The older computers were very inflexible, requiring a complete redesign of the network to change anything. Likewise, single-celled organisms such as bacteria can also afford to be inflexible, because they don't have to develop from embryos as multi-celled creatures do.

Mattick suggests that this new system somehow evolved (despite the irreducible complexity) and in turn enabled the evolution of many complex living things from simple organisms. The same evidence is better interpreted from a biblical framework — indeed this system can enable multicellular organisms to develop from a "simple" cell — but this is the fertilized egg. This makes more sense, since the fertilized egg has all the programming in place for all the information for a complex life form to develop from an embryo. It is also an example of good design economy pointing to a *single* Designer as opposed to many. In contrast, the first simple cell to evolve the complex splicing machinery would have no information to splice.

But Mattick may be partly right about diversification of life. Creationists also believe that life diversified — after the Flood. However, this diversification involved

11. Cooper, see reference 10.

no *new* information. Some creationists have proposed that certain parts of currently non-coding DNA could have enabled faster diversification,[12] and Mattick's theory could provide still another mechanism.

Evolutionists have produced a long list of examples of "bad design," but nothing on the list stands up under scrutiny.

---

12. E.g., T.C. Wood, altruistic genetic elements (AGEs), cited in Walkup, reference 7.

CHAPTER 8

ARGUMENT: THE FOSSIL RECORD SUPPORTS EVOLUTION

Evolutionists say, "Paleontologists have found
many examples of transitional fossils for
creatures such as birds, whales, and horses."

T his chapter discusses the fossil record, how interpretations are strongly influenced by one's assumptions, how it lacks the transitional forms evolution predicts, and discusses in detail some of the common evolutionary claims. Note: the human fossil record is not covered in this chapter, but in chapter 12.

THE FOSSIL RECORD: PREDICTION OF EVOLUTION?

Scientific American claims that the placement of fossils in the geologic record was predicted by evolution and is strong evidence for it. But it can't even keep the "facts" straight.

But one should not — and does not — find
modern human fossils embedded in strata from
the Jurassic period (65 million years ago). [*SA* 80]

Of course I don't believe the millions of years in the first place (see *The Young Earth*[1] for some reasons), but

1. John D. Morris, *The Young Earth* (Green Forest, AR: Master Books, Inc., 1994).

I know enough to know that *Scientific American* made a blooper even under its own perspective. Evolutionists assign the date of 65 Ma to the K–T (Cretaceous-Tertiary boundary), *not* to the Jurassic period. Instead, the Jurassic is dated after 208–144 Ma. After I first posted a rebuttal on the AiG website, *Scientific American* corrected their error on the web version of the article.

Actually, even if they found human fossils deeply buried in the earth that contradicted their assumptions about the geologic column and the fossil record, evolutionists could easily accommodate such "out of place fossils," as they have with living specimens of the "ancient" Coelacanth fish and "dinosaur era" Wollemi pine. These recent finds are just as sensational — from an evolutionary paleontologist's perspective — as finding a living dinosaur. Since the materialistic paradigm (interpretive framework) is all important, evolutionists would be able to explain an "old" human fossil by "reworking" (displacing from the initial burial depth), or maybe even reassigning such bones to another creature, since after all "we know" that humans can't be that deep in the fossil record!

A good example of reworking is the famous fossil footprints at Laetoli, Africa, of an upright walking biped — the University of Chicago's Dr. Russell Tuttle has shown that these are the same sorts of prints as made by habitually barefoot humans. But since they are dated at millions of years prior to when evolutionists believe modern humans arrived, they are regarded as australopithecine prints, by definition, even though australopithecine foot bones are substantially different from human ones. And then in an amazing twist, the same prints are held up as evidence that australopithecines walked upright like humans — regardless of the fact that other aspects of their anatomy indicate otherwise.[2]

In spite of evolutionists' assumptions to the contrary, the fossil order can be explained in a creationist framework, which actually avoids some of the contradictions of the evolutionary view.[3] The "fountains of the great deep" (Gen. 7:11) would logically have buried small seafloor creatures first. Water plants would generally be buried before coastal and mountain plants. Land creatures would be buried last, especially the mammals and birds that could escape to higher ground. The more intelligent creatures would find a way to escape until the very end, leaving their bodies nearer the surface, where post-Flood erosion would destroy most evidence of their existence. Humans would have been most resilient of all, clinging to debris and rafts, before they died of exposure; their floating bodies would have made easy meals for scavenging fish, so would not have fossilized as readily. Most mammal and human fossils are post-Flood.

ARGUMENT: MULTITUDES OF TRANSITIONAL FOSSILS EXIST

Evolutionists recognize a serious threat to their whole argument — evolution predicts innumerable transitional forms, yet all they have are a handful of debatable ones. Yet they are unwilling to admit to the magnitude of the problem. *Scientific American* states the problem in this way, and it answers with an unsupportable claim that there are numerous intermediate fossils.

---

2. Another good example of how a researcher's presuppositions can lead to all sorts of special pleading is the explaining away of clear evidence for a fossil belemnite. See T. Walker, "Fossil Flip-flop," *Creation* 22(1):6 (December 1999–February 2000).

3. See "Where Are All the Human Fossils?" <www.answersingenesis.org/docs2/4419.asp> and John Woodmorappe, "The Fossil Record: Becoming More Random All the Time," *TJ* 14(1):1002116 (December 1999–February 2000).

13. EVOLUTIONISTS CANNOT POINT TO ANY TRANSITIONAL FOSSILS — CREATURES THAT ARE HALF REPTILE AND HALF BIRD, FOR INSTANCE.

Actually, paleontologists know of many detailed examples of fossils intermediate in form between various taxonomic groups. [*SA* 83]

Actually, Charles Darwin was worried that the fossil record did not show what his theory predicted:

Why is not every geological formation and every stratum full of such intermediate links? Geology assuredly does not reveal any such finely-graduated organic chain; and this is the most obvious and serious objection which can be urged against the theory.[4]

More recently, Gould said:

The extreme rarity of transitional forms in the fossil record persists as the trade secret of paleontology.[5]

But modern evolutionists, including Gould, have asserted that there are nevertheless some transitional forms, but they always seem to name the same handful of disputable ones, instead of the many that Darwin hoped for. It's the same with *Scientific American* below.

Bird evolution

One of the most famous fossils of all time is *Archaeopteryx,* which combines feathers and skeletal structures peculiar to birds with features of dinosaurs. [*SA* 83]

4. C. Darwin, *Origin of Species*, 6th ed. 1872 (London: John Murray, 1902), p. 413.
5. S.J. Gould, "Evolution's Erratic Pace," *Natural History* 86(5):14, 1977.

The fossil bird known as *Archaeopteryx* is among the most prized relics in the world.

Artist's impression of *Archaeopteryx*, by Steve Cardno.

This hardly qualifies for a fossil "intermediate in form"; it is more like a mosaic or chimera like the platypus. Alan Feduccia, a world authority on birds at the University of North Carolina at Chapel Hill and an evolutionist himself, says:

> Paleontologists have tried to turn *Archaeopteryx* into an earth-bound, feathered dinosaur. But it's not. It is a bird, a perching bird. And no amount of "paleobabble" is going to change that.[6]

Archaeopteryx had fully-formed flying feathers (including asymmetric vanes and ventral, reinforcing furrows as in modern flying birds), the classical elliptical wings of modern woodland birds, and a large wishbone for attachment of muscles responsible for the down stroke of the wings.[7] Its brain was essentially that of a flying bird, with a large cerebellum and visual cortex.

6. Cited in V. Morell, *"Archaeopteryx*: Early Bird Catches a Can of Worms," *Science* 259(5096):764–65 (February 5, 1993).
7. A. Feduccia, "Evidence from Claw Geometry Indicating Arboreal Habits of *Archaeopteryx*," *Science* 259(5096):790–793 (February 5, 1993).

The fact that it had teeth is irrelevant to its alleged transitional status — a number of extinct birds had teeth, while many reptiles do not. Furthermore, like other birds, both its maxilla (upper jaw) and mandible (lower jaw) moved. In most vertebrates, including reptiles, only the mandible moves.[8] Finally, *Archaeopteryx* skeletons had pneumatized vertebrae and pelvis. This indicates the presence of both a cervical and abdominal air sac, i.e., at least two of the five sacs present in modern birds. This in turn indicates that the unique avian lung design was already present in what most evolutionists claim is the earliest bird.[9]

Scientific American hurls more elephants without examples.

> A flock's worth of other feathered fossil species, some more avian and some less, has also been found. [*SA* 83]

But the *Answers in Genesis* website has documented that two famous alleged feathered dinosaurs are "dated" younger than their supposed descendant, *Archaeopteryx,* and more likely to be flightless birds (*Protarchaeopteryx and Caudipteryx*). Another famous example, *Archaeoraptor*, was a fake.

Horse evolution

The horse sequence is another popular evidence of a fairly complete series of transitional fossils. *Scientific American* boldly claims:

> A sequence of fossils spans the evolution of modern horses from the tiny *Eohippus*. [*SA* 83]

8. See D. Menton with C. Wieland, "Bird Evolution Flies Out the Window," *Creation* 16(4):16–19 (June–August 1994).
9. P. Christiansen and N. Bonde, "Axial and Appendicular Pneumaticity in *Archaeopteryx*," *Proceedings of the Royal Society of London*, Series B. 267:2501–2505, 2000.

Like the *Archaeopteryx,* however, this doesn't hold up. Even informed evolutionists regard horse evolution as a bush rather than a sequence. But the so-called *Eohippus* is properly called *Hyracotherium,* and has little that could connect it with horses at all. The other animals in the "sequence" actually show hardly any more variation between them than that *within* horses today. One non-horse and many varieties of the true horse kind does not a sequence make.[10]

Mollusks

Scientific American makes another false claim:

Fossil seashells trace the evolution of various mollusks through millions of years. [*SA* 83]

Again, what does this mean? One must wonder if the author of the article believes the old *Ostrea/Gryphaea* story, i.e., that a flat oyster evolved into more and more coiled forms till it coiled itself shut. Once this was regarded as a key proof of an evolutionary lineage in the fossil record. But now it seems that the coiling was the oyster's built-in programming to respond to the environment, or *ecophenotypic change.*[11] So the anti-creationist neo-catastrophist geologist Derek Ager wrote:

It must be significant that nearly all the evolutionary stories I learned as a student, from Trueman's *Ostrea/Gryphaea* to Carruthers' *Zaphrentis delanouei,* have now been "debunked." Similarly, my own experience of more than twenty years looking for evolutionary lineages among the

---

10. See J. Sarfati, "The Non-evolution of the Horse," *Creation* 21(3):28–31 (June–August 1999).

11. M. Machalski, "Oyster Life Positions and Shell Beds from the Upper Jurassic of Poland," *Acta palaeontologica Polonica* 43(4):609–634, 1998. Abstract downloaded from <www.paleo.pan.pl/acta/acta43-4.htm#Machalski>, September 1, 2002.

Mesozoic Brachiopoda has proved them equally elusive.[12]

Scientific American closes its argument about transitional fossils with these mocking words about their demands for a truly transitional fossil:

> Creationists, though, dismiss these fossil studies. They argue that *Archaeopteryx* is not a missing link between reptiles and birds — it is just an extinct bird with reptilian features. They want evolutionists to produce a weird, chimeric monster that cannot be classified as belonging to any known group. [*SA* 83]

Actually, as stated, of the few transitional forms usually touted, most are actually chimeras. No, creationists have long simply requested a sequence of creatures with certain characteristics consistently following a series, e.g., 100% leg/0% wing → 90% leg/10% wing → ... 50% leg/ 50% wing ... → 10% leg/90% wing → 0% leg/100% wing.

> Even if a creationist does accept a fossil as transitional between two species, he or she may then insist on seeing other fossils intermediate between it and the first two. These frustrating requests can proceed *ad infinitum* and place an unreasonable burden on the always incomplete fossil record. [*SA* 83]

First, this again charges creationists with believing in fixity of species, which is rather a belief held by compromisers like Hugh Ross. Instead, creationists ask for transitions between major categories, such as between

---

12. D. Ager, "The Nature of the Fossil Record," *Proceedings of the Geologists' Association* 87(2):131–160, 1976; see also D. Catchpoole, "Evolution's Oyster Twist, *Creation* 24(2):55 (March–May 2002).

non-living matter and the first living cell, single-celled and multicelled creatures, and invertebrates and vertebrates. The gaps between these groups should be enough to show that molecules-to-man evolution is without foundation.

Second, this is hardly a new charge when made of fossils transitional between two phyla, for example, and it is hardly unreasonable for creationists to point out that there are still two large gaps rather than one even larger gap.[13]

WHALE EVOLUTION?

Whale evolution is a topic that deserves special attention. *Scientific American* claims:

> Whales had four-legged ancestors that walked on land, and creatures known as *Ambulocetus* and *Rodhocetus* helped to make that transition [see "The Mammals That Conquered the Seas," by Kate Wong, *Scientific American*, May]. [*SA* 83]

Here is an especially serious example of "hurling elephants" by completely ignoring the fragmentary nature of the evidence.

This was a tricky problem for Darwin, but nevertheless he still had faith that whales evolved from land mammals. The paleontologist Phil Gingerich of the University of Michigan has publicly said, "It's a real puzzle how whales originally evolved." But on the PBS *Evolution* series, he gives the impression that his fossil finds have gone a long way toward solving this puzzle.

Gingerich discovered in Pakistan a few skull fragments of a wolf-like creature that allegedly had an inner ear like a whale's. But this is far from conclusive. There

13. J. Woodmorappe, "Does a 'Transitional Form' Replace One Gap with Two Gaps?" *TJ* 14(2):5–6, 2000.

Pakicetus: "Evidence" for Whale Evolution?

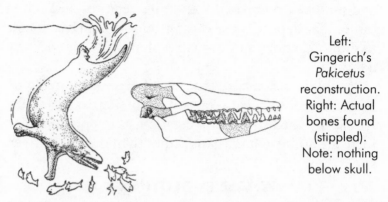

Left: Gingerich's *Pakicetus* reconstruction. Right: Actual bones found (stippled). Note: nothing below skull.

Left: J. Gingerich, *Geol. Educ.* 31:140–144, 1983; right: Gingerich et al., *Science* 220: 403–6, 1983.

wasn't any post-cranial skeleton found, so we haven't the faintest idea how it moved. However, this didn't stop Gingerich from writing an article for schoolteachers with an illustration of an animal that had splashed into the sea and was swimming and catching fish, and looking convincingly like an intermediate between land animals and whales. He also claimed, "In time and in its morphology, *Pakicetus* is perfectly intermediate, a missing link between earlier land mammals and later, full-fledged whales."[14] The diagram above shows the glaring contrast between reconstruction and reality.

New research since the PBS series was produced has blown away this reconstruction. This demonstrates an oft-repeated phenomenon in evolutionary paleontology. Many of the alleged transitional forms are based on fragmentary remains, which are therefore open to several interpretations, based on one's axioms. Evolutionary bias means that such remains are often likely to be interpreted as transitional, as with Gingerich, and is also prevalent in ape-man claims. But when more bones are discovered,

14. P. Gingerich, "The Whales of Tethys," *Natural History* (April 1994): p. 86.

Pakicetus

Illustration: Carl Buell <http://www.neoucom.edu/Depts/Anat/Pakicetid.html>

then the fossils nearly always fit one type or another, and are no longer plausible as transitional. It's also notable that alleged intermediate forms are often trumpeted in the media, while retractions are usually muted or unpublicized.

A prominent whale expert, Thewissen, and colleagues unearthed some more bones of *Pakicetus*, and published their work in the journal *Nature*.[15] The commentary on this paper in the same issue says, "All the postcranial bones indicate that pakicetids were land mammals, and . . . indicate that the animals were runners, with only their feet touching the ground" (see illustration above).[16] This is very different from Gingerich's picture of an aquatic animal! But the evolutionary bias is still clear, describing *Pakicetus* as a "terrestrial cetacean" and saying, "The first whales were fully terrestrial, and were even efficient runners." But the term "whale" becomes meaningless if it can describe land mammals, and it provides no insight into how true marine whales supposedly evolved.

---

15. J.G.M. Thewissen, E.M. Williams, L.J. Roe, and S.T. Hussain, "Skeletons of Terrestrial Cetaceans and the Relationship of Whales to Artiodactyls," *Nature* 413:277–281 (September 20, 2001).
16. C. de Muizon, "Walking with Whales," *Nature* 413:259–260 (September 20, 2001), comment on reference 15.

Also, "solid anatomical data" contradict previous theories of whale ancestry. A Reuters news article reported in September 2001:

> Until now paleontologists thought whales had evolved from mesonychians, an extinct group of land-dwelling carnivores, while molecular scientists studying DNA were convinced they descended from artiodactyls [even-toed ungulates].[17]

"The paleontologists, and I am one of them, were wrong," Gingerich said.

Such candor is commendable, and it shows the fallacy of trusting alleged "proofs" of evolution. Pity that Gingerich is still committed to materialistic evolutionism.

Ambulocetus

Ambulocetus is another popular example of a "missing link," featured prominently in anti-creationist propaganda, such as the book *Finding Darwin's God*, by Kenneth Miller — the "Christian evolutionist" who starred in PBS 1. In his book, Miller claimed, "the animal could move easily both on land and in water," and presented a drawing of a complete skeleton and a reconstructed animal.[18] But this is misleading, bordering on deceitful, and indicative of Miller's unreliability, because there was no indication of the fact that far fewer bones were actually found than appear in his diagram. Crucially, the all-important pelvic girdle was not found (see diagram at top of following page). Without this, it's presumptuous for Miller to make that proclamation. His fellow evolutionist, Annalisa Berta, pointed out:

---

17. "Fossil Finds Show Whales Related to Early Pigs," *Reuters* (September 19, 2001), <www.spectrum.ieee.org/news/cache/ReutersOnlineScience/09_19_2001.romta1708-story-bcsciencesciencewhalesdc.html>.
18. Kenneth R. Miller, *Finding Darwin's God* (New York, NY: Cliff Street Books, 1999), p. 265.

Ambulocetus: Missing Link?

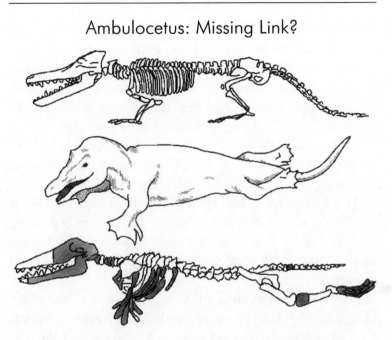

Top: *Ambulocetus* skeleton, as drawn in Miller's book.
Middle: *Ambulocetus* reconstruction, as drawn in Miller's book.
Bottom: Actual bones found (shaded). Note missing pelvic girdle.

. . . since the pelvic girdle is not preserved, there is no direct evidence in *Ambulocetus* for a connection between the hind limbs and the axial skeleton. This hinders interpretations of locomotion in this animal, since many of the muscles that support and move the hindlimb originate on the pelvis.[19]

---

19. A. Berta, "What Is a Whale?" *Science* 263(5144):180–181, 1994; perspective on J.G.M. Thewissen, S.T. Hussain, and M. Arif, "Fossil Evidence for the Origin of Aquatic Locomotion in Archeocete Whales," same issue, p. 210—212; see also D. Batten, "A Whale of a Tale?" *TJ* 8(1):2–3, 1994; the online version <www.answersingenesis.org/ambulo>, includes the addendum addressing claims of subsequent *Ambulocetus* bones and their (ir)relevance to evolution.

Basilosaurus

This serpentine and fully aquatic mammal has been known since the 19th century, but Gingerich discovered something new in some specimens in the Sahara. The PBS narrator pointed out that this desert area was under water once, and he described a 100-mile stretch of layered sandstone called the "valley of the whales" allegedly 40 million years old. The narrator theorizes that this valley was once a protected bay where whales came to give birth and to die. Here Gingerich discovered what he alleged were a pelvis, leg bones, and a knee cap, so he said they were evidence of "functioning legs" and "dramatic proof that whales were once fully four-legged mammals."

But this contradicts other evolutionists, including Gingerich himself! For example, the National Academy of Science's *Teaching about Evolution and the Nature of Science* claimed, "they were thought to be nonfunctional" (p. 18), and Gingerich himself said elsewhere "it seems to me that they could only have been some kind of sexual and reproductive clasper."[20] So these bones can be explained as a design feature, while the interpretation as "legs" reflects evolutionary wishful thinking.[21]

Whale evolutionary sequence?

The PBS program claims that there is a series including *Ambulocetus, Rhodocetus,* etc., where the nostrils supposedly migrate to the back of the head. *Teaching about Evolution and the Nature of Science* contains a diagram (see following page) on page 18. But when the mammal-to-whale series is examined, the sequence is not as

---

20. *Press Enterprise* (1 July 1, 1990): A-15.
21. Another urban myth about whales found with legs is punctured in C. Wieland, "The Strange Tale of the Leg on the Whale," *Creation* 20(3):10–13 (September–November 1998).

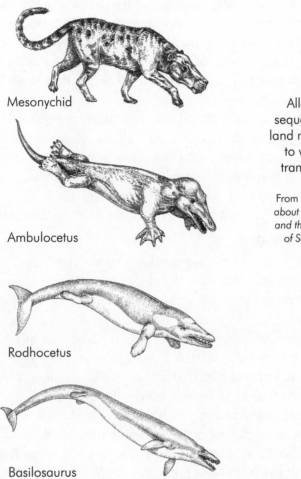

Mesonychid

Ambulocetus

Rodhocetus

Basilosaurus

Alleged
sequence of
land mammal
to whale
transition.

From *Teaching
about Evolution
and the Nature
of Science*.

smooth as they imply. For instance, this diagram failed
to indicate that *Basilosaurus* is actually about ten times
longer than *Ambulocetus* (and the fragmentary nature
of the remains has been discussed already).

Another problem is that *Basilosaurus* has a number
of features that mean it could not possibly have been
ancestral to modern whales, e.g., body shape, skull structure, and tooth shape.

There is certainly no support for the program's claim, "front legs became fins, rear legs disappeared, bodies lost fur and took on their familiar streamlined shape." Waving the magic wand of mutation/selection is hardly sufficient without an observable *mechanism* that would effect these changes.

Recently, John Woodmorappe analyzed the alleged transitions and found that their various characteristics did not change in a consistent direction. Rather, they are chimeras — non-whales with a few minor cetacean "modules," inconsistent with the evolutionary prediction of a nested hierarchy but consistent with a *common Designer*.[22]

Locomotion

PBS 2 also claims support for a transition from the way the mammal-to-whale fossil links moved. Marine mammals move through the water with vertical undulating movements of the spine, just as many fast-running mammals do on land. Fish move with sideways undulations instead. But this could be another common design feature of mammals, like milk or hair. It's also doubtful whether this is a unique prediction of evolution; if whales used side-to-side movements, evolutionists could presumably have "predicted" this because the tails of land animals also swish sideways.

My book, *Refuting Evolution*, written to rebut *Teaching about Evolution and the Nature of Science,* has a chapter on alleged whale evolution that covers all this section in more detail, with full documentation. It is also available on the *Creation* CD produced by Answers in Genesis in answer to the PBS series.

TETRAPOD EVOLUTION?

Tetrapods are animals with four limbs, i.e., amphibians, reptiles, birds, and mammals. In 1995, Shubin and

22. J. Woodmorappe, "Walking Whales, Nested Hierarchies and Chimeras: Do They Exist?" *TJ* 16(1):111–119, 2002.

Deschler found in Pennsylvanian cliffs a shoulder bone of a tetrapod allegedly 370 million years old.

Cambridge University paleontologist Jenny Clack found an early tetrapod hand in Greenland, called *Acanthostega*. Supposedly, this creature had gills, a fish-like tail, paddle-shaped fins, and a hand with fingers.

On PBS 2, Clack said this refuted the usual textbook theory that fish evolved limbs for a selective advantage because they were being stranded in drying pools. Rather, the limbs evolved before they crawled on the land, while they were still aquatic. The selective advantage was the ability to escape the weird and wonderful predatory fish that lived during this time (called the Devonian Period).

Shubin stressed that "evolution wasn't trying to do this," and later the PBS program claimed, "we're here through chance coincidences." This should make it clear that evolution, as believed by evolutionists, is not "progressive" and shows no sign of a divine guiding hand.

Shubin also highlighted the common limb pattern between tetrapods, illustrated by fish and humans having the sequence one bone/two bones/small bones/rods (digits). But this fails to explain the totally different developmental sequence, as previously explained (chapter 6).

CAMBRIAN EXPLOSION

During his appearance on PBS 2, Cambridge University paleontologist Simon Conway Morris explained that the Cambrian explosion was "one of the greatest breakthroughs in the history of life." Essentially all the different animal phyla (major groups) appeared abruptly, without any known transitional forms preceding them. According to evolutionary dating methods, this was about 500 million years ago. Morris acknowledged that Darwin recognized this as a problem for his theory, with animals appearing out of nowhere. Morris said, "To a certain extent that is still a mystery." Darwin predicted that animals diverged gradually from a common pattern, so there should be fossil examples of this divergence, while instead we see that the major differences arose abruptly at the beginning. Again, this is according to the evolutionary time frame; biblical creationists see the fossil record not as a time sequence but a sequence of burial by Noah's flood and its after-effects.

Then the PBS program shifted to the Burgess Shale, with lots of bizarre creatures, e.g., one with five eyes, another worm-like creature with large spines, and still another with prongs around its mouth. But none of this showed what the Cambrian animals could have evolved from. Supposedly the evidence shows that evolution tinkered with a few basic body plans, but provides no evidence for their *origins*.

It should also be noted that, when geologists say life appeared suddenly during the Cambrian explosion without transitional forms, they're making a backhand admission of the paucity of transitional fossils.

EXTINCTION!

The whole emphasis on extinction, such as PBS 3 on "Extinction!" is rather strange. It hardly tells us anything to prove evolution *per se*. Rather, it says a lot about species *dying out*, which is hardly news to anyone, but it doesn't itself shed any light on how species *arose* in the first place. The PBS program makes plenty of *assertions* about new species diversifying to take the place of the old ones, but it offers no *evidence* of any mechanism by which this could occur. It's just another example of how vacuous words can become when survivors of extinctions are called "evolution's big winners." How exactly does the word "evolution" explain anything here? The only purpose seems to be to further the indoctrination of the public with the idea that it does. But really, saying "history's big winners" or "winners of the lottery of life" would be just as informative.

Have most species become extinct?

PBS 3 repeated the common claim that 95–99 percent of species have become extinct. However, the *known* record of extinct and extant species does not support this. The number of fossil species *actually found* is estimated to be about 250,000, while there are about three million living "species," or even more, depending on who's telling the story. But if this >95% claim were correct, we would expect many more fossil species than living ones.

The only plausible explanation is evolutionary bias. For evolution to be true, there would have been innumerable transitional forms between different types of creatures. Therefore, for every known fossil species, many more must have existed to connect it to its ancestors and descendents. This is yet another example of evolutionary conclusions coming before the evidence. Really, the claim is an implicit admission that large numbers of transitional forms are predicted, which heightens the difficulty for evolutionists, given how few there are that even they could begin to claim were candidates.

Mass extinctions

Supposedly there were five mass extinctions in earth's history, caused by planet-wide catastrophes. The greatest was the Permian extinction about 250 million years ago, where 90 percent of species became extinct. The period allegedly represented by rock layers above the Permian, the Triassic, was almost void of life. But later, in the upper Triassic, the dinosaurs supposedly evolved. Alongside them were the mammal-like reptiles that supposedly evolved into mammals.

The best-known extinction was alleged to be that of the dinosaurs, at the end of the Cretaceous, dated at 65 million years ago. Supposedly the small mammals, who kept out of sight when dinosaurs were around, managed to survive the catastrophe by hiding in burrows, while dinosaurs couldn't hide or protect their eggs. In the next period, the Tertiary, mammals are supposed to have diversified and filled the vacant niches.

The PBS program presents the usual meteorite impact theory as fact, i.e., a chunk of rock the size of Mt. Everest hit earth at 25,000 mph. The many problems with this idea are ignored. For example:

- The extinction was not that sudden (using evolutionary/long-age interpretations of the geological record). But the spread in the geological record makes sense if much of the sedimentary deposits were formed in Noah's flood.
- Light-sensitive species survived.
- Extinctions don't correlate with crater dates, even given evolutionary dating assumptions.
- Modern volcanic eruptions don't cause global extinction patterns, even if they cause a temporary temperature drop.
- The iridium enrichment, supposedly a key proof of meteor impact, is not nearly as clearly defined as claimed.
- Drill cores of the apparent "smoking gun" crater on the Yucatán peninsula in southeast Mexico do not support the idea that it is an impact crater.
- It seems that some scientists didn't speak out against the idea for fear of undermining the "nuclear winter" idea, and being grouped with "nuclear warmongers."[23]

---

23. See my analysis in "Did a Meteor Wipe Out the Dinosaurs? What about the Iridium Layer?" <www.answersingenesis.org/iridium>; after Charles Officer and Jake Page, *The Great Dinosaur Extinction Controversy* (Reading, MA: Addison-Wesley, 1996), reviewed by C. Wieland, *TJ* 12(2):154–158, 1998.

In general, mass extinctions are explained as a house of cards collapsing, where each card represents a species. One species may collapse, but then all other species that depend on it, either directly or indirectly, will also collapse. Even without a catastrophe, there are many factors that can cause a "bottom card" species to die out, e.g., a new predator or climatic change.

Why bother preserving species?

All of this talk about fossils and extinctions causes a problem for evolutionists who are also rabid environmental extremists. The PBS episode on extinction exposes this problem: first, it asserts that humans are just another species, then it insists that extinction is simply part of earth's history, and finally it moralizes that humans should try to preserve other species. The narrator says that humans "may be the asteroid that brings about the next mass extinction," and that we "competed with other species and won."

But if we're just another species, then why shouldn't we act like one? Why should we aid our competitors for survival, when other species act in self-interest? The only reason might be a practical one, that we might lose some species that are beneficial to us. But this is very different from a *moral obligation* to care for them. If we are all rearranged pond scum, then talk of moral obligation is meaningless. Under a consistent evolutionary worldview, our moral sentiments are merely chemical motions in the brain that happened to confer a survival advantage in our alleged ape-like ancestors.

Creationist explanation

As elaborated earlier, the Bible teaches that death is the "last enemy," the result of Adam's sin, and is an intruder into God's very good creation. This is a problem for those who want to add millions of years to the Bible, and this program demonstrated just how much death is entailed by millions-of-years belief, because of the record of death (and disease, violence, etc.) the fossils portray.

Biblical creationists would explain much of the fossil record by the global flood of Noah's day. However, this didn't directly cause any land vertebrates to become extinct, because each kind was represented on the ark.[24] But many became extinct in subsequent centuries, because of factors already well known to conservationists.[25] But the Flood probably did cause many marine species to become extinct.

Creationists and evolutionists interpret the geological layers differently because of our different axioms. Evolutionists interpret the sequence of layers as a sequence of *ages* with different types of creatures; creationists interpret them as a sequence of *burial* by a global flood and its after-effects. This makes better sense of phenomena such as "living fossils" and finding creatures such as the coelacanth, which isn't found in rocks "dated" younger than 70 million years.

24. J. Sarfati, "How Did All the Animals Fit on Noah's Ark?" *Creation* 19(2):16–19 (March–May 1997); J. Woodmorappe, *Noah's Ark: A Feasibility Study* (El Cajon, CA: Institute for Creation Research, 1996).
25. K. Ham, *The Great Dinosaur Mystery Solved!* details the history of the dinosaurs from a biblical perspective (Green Forest, AR: Master Books, Inc., 1998).

3

CLAIM: "PROBLEMS" WITH EVOLUTION ARE ILLUSORY

Evolutionists argue that there are reasonable theories for even the biggest "surprises" of evolution.

CHAPTER 9

ARGUMENT: PROBABILITY OF EVOLUTION

Evolutionists say, "Biochemistry, computer simulations, and observations of 'natural' order (such as crystals and snowflakes) show that evolution is highly probable."

This chapter will examine several claims about the probability of evolution. I'll quote from points 7, 8, and 9 of *Scientific American*'s "15 Answers to Creationist Nonsense," and then respond in turn. Each point in *Scientific American* gives a charge against evolution, followed by the magazine's attempted answer.

ORIGIN OF LIFE

7. EVOLUTION CANNOT EXPLAIN HOW LIFE FIRST APPEARED ON EARTH.

The origin of life remains very much a mystery, but biochemists have learned about how primitive nucleic acids, amino acids, and other building blocks of life could have formed. . . . [*SA* 81]

Actually, they have found out how some major building blocks CANNOT be formed, e.g., cytosine. The proposed "prebiotic" conditions that biochemists attempt to recreate in the laboratory are unrealistic because it is highly unlikely that the alleged "precursor chemicals" could ever have concentrated sufficiently, and these chemicals would have undergone side reactions with other organic compounds. Cytosine is far too unstable, anyway, to have accumulated over "deep time" because its half life is only 340 years at $25°$ C.[1]

. . . and organized themselves into self-replicating, self-sustaining units. . . . [SA 81]

This is just bluff, since spontaneous polymerization is a major hurdle for non-living chemicals to overcome.[2] So is producing molecules all of one handedness.[3] Chemical evolutionists have yet to solve these problems, let alone produce any self-replicating system which has any relevance to cells.[4]

. . . laying the foundation for cellular biochemistry. Astrochemical analyses hint that quantities of these compounds might have originated in space and fallen to earth in comets, a scenario that may solve the problem of how those constituents arose under the conditions that prevailed when our planet was young. [SA 81]

Again, wishful thinking, partly motivated by the hopelessness of current theories about life spontaneously

1. J. Sarfati, "Origin of Life: Instability of Building Blocks," *TJ* 13(2):124–127, 1999.
2. J. Sarfati, "Origin of Life: The Polymerization Problem," *TJ* 12(3):281–284, 1998.
3. J. Sarfati, "Origin of Life: The Chirality Problem," *TJ* 12(3):263–266, 1998.
4. J. Sarfati, "Self-Replicating Enzymes?" *TJ* 11(1):4–6, 1997.

generating on earth. There are several problems, including the following:[5]

- The amounts of these chemicals are tiny — far too low to contribute to biological processes.

- The wide variety of compounds in itself counts as evidence against chemical evolution. Even with pure compounds used in experiments, the results are meager, so how much worse would they be with the contaminated gunk produced in the real world?

- Sugars are very unstable, and easily decompose or react with other chemicals. This counts against any proposed mechanism to concentrate them to useable proportions.

- Living things require homochiral sugars, i.e., with the same handedness, but the ones from space would not have been.

- Even under highly artificial conditions, there is no plausible method of making the sugar ribose join to some of the essential building blocks needed to make DNA or RNA. Instead, the tendency is for long molecules to break down.

- Even DNA or RNA by themselves would not constitute life, since it's not enough just to join the bases ("letters") together, but the sequence must be meaningful — and this sequence is not a function of the chemistry of the letters.

- Even the correct letter sequence would be meaningless without elaborate decoding machinery to translate it. Unless the decoding machinery already existed, those instructions could never be read. Similarly, this

5. J. Sarfati, "Sugars from Space? Do They Prove Evolution?" *TJ* 16(1):9–11, 2002; "Did Life's Building Blocks Come from Outer Space? Amino Acids from Interstellar Simulation Experiments?" *TJ* 16(2):17–20, 2002.

book would be useless to a non-English-speaker, who may know the Roman alphabet but lacks knowledge of the code of the *English* language to convert letters into meaningful concepts.

The *Scientific American* article continues:

> Creationists sometimes try to invalidate all of evolution by pointing to science's current inability to explain the origin of life. But even if life on earth turned out to have a non-evolutionary origin (for instance, if aliens introduced the first cells billions of years ago), evolution since then would be robustly confirmed by countless microevolutionary and macroevolutionary studies. [*SA* 81]

Here we go again with the bait'n'switch concerning the meanings of evolution. Anyway, that downplays the real problem. Evolution is a pseudo-intellectual justification for materialism, because it purports to explain life without God. So materialism would be in great trouble if evolution had a problem right at the start ("chemical evolution"). After all, if the process can't even start, it can't continue.

EVOLUTION "DOES NOT DEPEND ON CHANCE"? REALLY?

8. MATHEMATICALLY, IT IS INCONCEIVABLE THAT ANYTHING AS COMPLEX AS A PROTEIN, LET ALONE A LIVING CELL OR A HUMAN, COULD SPRING UP BY CHANCE.

> Chance plays a part in evolution (for example, in the random mutations that can give rise to new traits), but evolution does not depend on chance to create organisms, proteins, or other entities. Quite the

opposite: natural selection, the principal known mechanism of evolution, harnesses nonrandom change by preserving "desirable" (adaptive) features and eliminating "undesirable" (nonadaptive) ones. [*SA* 81]

But the raw material on which natural selection acts is random copying errors (mutations). If evolution by goo-to-you were true, we should expect to find *countless* information-adding mutations. But we have not even found *one*.

It is misleading to claim that evolution does not depend on chance but instead it relies on "non-random" natural selection. This ignores the fact that natural selection cannot explain the *origin* of *complex,* self-reproducing life forms — and evolutionists have no way to explain this essential step in the evolution of life.

Incidentally, it's important to note that a *non-complex* life form is an impossibility, since it needs to have the ability to reproduce. Even the simplest known true self-reproducing organism, *Mycoplasma genitalium* (a parasitic bacterium, discussed in chapter 4), has 482 genes with 580,000 "letters" (base pairs). But even this appears not to be enough to sustain itself without parasitizing an even more complex organism. Most likely, as discussed, the parasitism resulted from loss of some of the genetic information required to make some essential nutrients.[6] Therefore, a hypothetical first cell that could sustain itself would have to be even *more* complex.

As long as the forces of selection stay constant, natural selection can push evolution in one direction and produce sophisticated structures in surprisingly short times. [*SA* 81]

An *example* would have been nice.

---

6. T.C. Wood, "Genome Decay in the Mycoplasmas," *Impact* 340 (October 2001); <www.icr.org/pubs/imp/imp-340.htm>.

COMPUTER "SIMULATIONS" OF EVOLUTION

Scientific American alludes to computer "simulations" of evolution, although these are based on assumptions that do *not* parallel real life:

> As an analogy, consider the 13-letter sequence "TOBEORNOTTOBE." Those hypothetical million monkeys, each pecking out one phrase a second, could take as long as 78,800 years to find it among the 2,613 sequences of that length. But in the 1980s, Richard Hardison of Glendale College wrote a computer program that generated phrases randomly while preserving the positions of individual letters that happened to be correctly placed (in effect, selecting for phrases more like Hamlet's). On average, the program re-created the phrase in just 336 iterations, less than 90 seconds. Even more amazing, it could reconstruct Shakespeare's entire play in just four and a half days. [*SA* 81–82]

These computer programs have been widely popularized by the atheist Richard Dawkins, but are a lot of bluff. Such simulations, which Dawkins and, now, *Scientific American* propose as "simulations" of evolution, work toward a known goal, so they are far from a parallel to real evolution, which has no foresight, hence a "Blind Watchmaker." The simulations also use "organisms" with high reproductive rates (producing many offspring), high mutation rates, a large probability of a beneficial mutation, and a selection coefficient of 1 (perfect selection) instead of 0.01 (or less), which parallels real life more accurately. The "organisms" have tiny "genomes" with minute information content, so they are less prone to error catastrophe, and they are not affected by the chemical and thermodynamic constraints of a real organism.

TJ published an article about a realistic computer simulation, with a program downloadable from the AiG website,[7] which shows that the goal is *not* reached if realistic values are programmed, or it takes so long that it shows that evolution is impossible.[8]

Also, when it comes to the origin of *first* life, natural selection cannot be invoked, because natural selection is differential reproduction. That is, if it worked at all, it could only work on a living organism that could produce offspring. By its very definition, it could not work on non-living chemicals.[9] Therefore, chance *alone* must produce the precise sequences needed, so these simulations do not apply. And a further problem with the alleged chemical soup is reversibility, intensifying the difficulty of obtaining the right sequence by chance.[10]

RANDOM ORDER ≠ COMPLEXITY

Scientific American's next example of "creationist nonsense" begins with shadow boxing against an argument that informed creationists don't make (see appendix on the second law of thermodynamics). Then the

7. D. Batten and L. Ey, "Weasel, a Flexible Program for Investigating Deterministic Computer 'Demonstrations' of Evolution," *TJ* 16(2):84–88, 2002; <www.answersingenesis.org/weasel>.
8. For more information, see my refutation of Dawkins's book, *Climbing Mt. Improbable, Stumbling Over the Impossible, TJ* 12(1):29–34, 1998; <www.answersingenesis.org/dawkins>. Also see W. Gitt with C. Wieland, "Weasel Words," *Creation* 20(4):20–21 (September–November 1998), and R. Truman, "Dawkins's Weasel Revisited," *TJ* 12(3):358–361, 1998. For a refutation of the whole idea of computer simulations of evolution, particularly in the guise of genetic algorithms, see Don Batten, "Genetic Algorithms — Do They Show That Evolution Works?" <www.answersingenesis.org/ga>. All these problems also apply to the simplistic "simulation" *Scientific American* writes about.
9. Sidney Fox, editor, *The Origins of Prebiological Systems,* "Synthesis of Nucleosides and Polynucleotides with Metaphosphate Esters," T. Dobzhansky (New York, NY: Academic Press, 1965).
10. R. Grigg, "Could Monkeys Type the 23rd Psalm?" *Creation* 13(1):30–33 (December 1990–February 1991); <www.answersingenesis.org/monkeys>.

article proceeds to reveal a common mistake that evolutionists make: assuming that the random occurrence of *order* (repetitive, low information) in nature, such as crystals and snowflakes, provides insight into the generation of *complexity* (nonrepetitive, high information).

9. THE SECOND LAW OF THERMODYNAMICS SAYS THAT SYSTEMS MUST BECOME MORE DISORDERED OVER TIME. LIVING CELLS THEREFORE COULD NOT HAVE EVOLVED FROM INANIMATE CHEMICALS, AND MULTICELLULAR LIFE COULD NOT HAVE EVOLVED FROM PROTOZOA.

> This argument derives from a misunderstanding of the Second Law. [*SA* 82]

It would be most surprising, in our experience, if an anti-creationist lacking training in physics or chemistry understood the second law himself. As will be shown, biologist John Rennie, who wrote the *Scientific American* article on "creationist nonsense," is no exception. I should say that Rennie's formulation of the creationist argument is not how informed creationists would argue — see appendix.

> If it were valid, mineral crystals and snowflakes would also be impossible, because they, too, are complex structures that form spontaneously from disordered parts. [*SA* 82]

No, as usual, this anti-creationist confuses *order* with complexity. The difference between crystals in rocks and proteins in living organisms is profound. Break a crystal and you just get smaller crystals; break a protein and you don't simply get a smaller protein; rather you lose the function completely. Large crystals have low information content that is simply repeated, while the protein molecule isn't constructed simply by repetition. Those who manufacture proteins know that they have to add one amino acid at a time, and each addition has about 90 chemical steps involved.

> The Second Law actually states that the total entropy of a closed system (one that no energy or matter leaves or enters). . . . [SA 82]

It's more usual for those qualified in physical chemistry to refer to this as an *isolated system*, and use the term *closed system* for one where energy, but not matter, can be exchanged with its surroundings.

> . . . cannot decrease. Entropy is a physical concept often casually described as disorder, but it differs significantly from the conversational use of the word. [SA 82]

We totally agree, and point this out often.

> More important, however, the Second Law permits parts of a system to decrease in entropy as long as other parts experience an offsetting increase. Thus, our planet as a whole can grow more complex because the sun pours heat and light onto it, and the greater entropy associated with the sun's nuclear fusion more than rebalances the scales. Simple organisms can fuel their rise toward complexity by consuming other forms of life and nonliving materials. [SA 82]

This energy input is necessary *but not sufficient*. The proverbial bull in a china shop produces disorder, but if the same bull was harnessed to a generator, this energy could be directed into useful work. Similarly, living organisms have machinery to direct the energy from sunlight or food, including the ATP synthase enzyme. This is the world's tiniest motor, so tiny that 10^{17} could fit into a pinhead.[11] Paul Boyer and John Walker won a half share of the 1997 Nobel Prize for Chemistry for their proposal that the enzyme was a motor after the research in reference 11 (*Nature* articles) confirmed it. But machinery presupposes teleology (purpose), which means that the machinery must have had an intelligent source.

11. H. Noji et al., "Direct Observation of the Rotation of F1-ATPase." *Nature* 386(6622):299–302, 1997. Comment by S. Block, "Real Engines of Creation," same issue, p. 217–219; J. Sarfati, "Design in Living Organisms: Motors," *TJ* 12(1):3–5, 1998, <www.answersingenesis.org\motor>.

CHAPTER 10

ARGUMENT: "IRREDUCIBLE COMPLEXITY"

Evolutionists say, "Examples of supposed 'irreducible complexity' (such as the eye, the complex cell and the flagellum) can be explained."

This chapter will examine how evolutionists respond to the "irreducible complexity" argument in three areas: the eye, the complex cell and the flagellum. *Scientific American* states the problem this way:

14. LIVING THINGS HAVE FANTASTICALLY INTRICATE FEATURES — AT THE ANATOMICAL, CELLULAR AND MOLECULAR LEVELS — THAT COULD NOT FUNCTION IF THEY WERE ANY LESS COMPLEX OR SOPHISTICATED. THE ONLY PRUDENT CONCLUSION IS THAT THEY ARE THE PRODUCTS OF INTELLIGENT DESIGN, NOT EVOLUTION.

This "argument from design" is the backbone of most recent attacks on evolution, but it is also one of the oldest. In 1802, theologian William

Paley wrote that if one finds a pocket watch in a field, the most reasonable conclusion is that someone dropped it, not that natural forces created it there. By analogy, Paley argued, the complex structures of living things must be the handiwork of direct, divine invention. Darwin wrote *On the Origin of Species* as an answer to Paley: he explained how natural forces of selection, acting on inherited features, could gradually shape the evolution of ornate organic structures. [*SA* 83]

Indeed, Gould, who was an expert on the history of evolution, agreed that Darwin was writing to counter Paley. This is another way of saying that he had an antitheistic agenda,[1] as discussed in chapter 2. This doesn't stop many churchian academics kowtowing to every pronouncement made by Darwin and his God-hating successors, who in return regard them as contemptuously as Lenin regarded his "useful idiot" allies in the West.[2]

COULD THE EYE HAVE EVOLVED?

It's interesting to note that the eye, which evolutionists claim is an example of "bad design" leftover from evolution (previous chapter), presents their greatest challenge as an example of superb "irreducible complexity" in God's creation. *Scientific American* says:

Generations of creationists have tried to counter Darwin by citing the example of the eye as a structure that could not have evolved. The eye's ability to provide vision depends on the perfect arrangement of its parts, these critics say.

1. Carl Wieland, "Darwin's Real Message: Have You Missed It?" *Creation* 14(4):16–19 (September–November 1992); J. Sarfati, review of K. Birkett, *The Essence of Darwinism* <www.answersingenesis.org/birkett>.
2. J. Sarfati, "The Skeptics and Their 'Churchian' Allies," <www.answersingenesis.org/docs/3906.asp>.

Natural selection could thus never favor the transitional forms needed during the eye's evolution — what good is half an eye? Anticipating this criticism, Darwin suggested that even "incomplete" eyes might confer benefits (such as helping creatures orient toward light) and thereby survive for further evolutionary refinement. [*SA* 83]

First, this overlooks the incredible complexity of even the simplest light-sensitive spot. Second, it's fallacious to argue that 51 percent vision would necessarily have a strong enough selective advantage over 50 percent to overcome the effects of genetic drift's tendency to eliminate even beneficial mutations.[3]

Biology has vindicated Darwin: researchers have identified primitive eyes and light-sensing organs throughout the animal kingdom and have even tracked the evolutionary history of eyes through comparative genetics. (It now appears that in various families of organisms, eyes have evolved independently.) [*SA* 83]

Scientific American contradicts itself here. If the evolutionary history of eyes has been tracked through comparative genetics, how is it that eyes have supposedly evolved independently? Actually, evolutionists recognize that eyes must have arisen independently at least 30 times because there is no evolutionary pattern to explain the origin of eyes from a common ancestor. What this really means is that since eyes cannot be related by common ancestor, and since they are here, and only materialistic

---

3. See my discussion about the evolution of the eye in "Stumbling Over the Impossible: Refutation of Climbing Mt. Improbable," *TJ* 12(1):29–34, 1998; <www.answersingenesis.org/dawkins#eye>.

explanations are allowed, hey presto, there's proof that they evolved independently!

SIMULATION OF EYE EVOLUTION

PBS 1 goes to great lengths to convince us that the eye could easily have evolved. Dan Nilsson explained a simplistic computer simulation he published in a widely publicized paper.[4] Taking his cue from Darwin, who started with a light-sensitive spot when "explaining" the origin of the eye, Nilsson's simulation starts with a light-sensitive layer, with a transparent coating in front and a light-absorbing layer behind.

Here is how the simulation proceeds. Firstly, the light-sensitive layer bends gradually into a cup, so it can tell the direction of light rays increasingly well. This continues until it is curved into a hemisphere filled with the transparent substance. Secondly, bringing the ends together, closing the aperture, gradually increases the sharpness of the image, as a pinhole camera does, because a smaller hole cuts out light. But because of the diffraction of light if the hole is too small, there is a limit to this process. So thirdly, the shape and refractive index gradient of the transparent cover change gradually to a finely focusing lens. Even if we were generous and presumed that such computer simulations really have anything to do with the real world of biochemistry, there are more serious problems.

However, the biochemist Michael Behe has shown that even a "simple" light-sensitive spot requires a dazzling array of biochemicals in the right place and time to function. He states that each of its "cells makes the complexity of a motorcycle or television set look

---

4. D.E. Nilsson and S. Pelger, "A Pessimistic Estimate of the Time Required for an Eye to Evolve," *Proc. R. Soc. Lond.* B 256:53–58, 1994.

paltry in comparison" and describes a small part of what's involved:[5]

When light first strikes the retina a photon interacts with a molecule called 11-*cis*-retinal, which rearranges within picoseconds to *trans*-retinal. (A picosecond [10^{-12} sec] is about the time it takes light to travel the breadth of a single human hair.) The change in the shape of the retinal molecule forces a change in the shape of the protein, rhodopsin, to which the retinal is tightly bound. The protein's metamorphosis alters its behavior. Now called metarhodopsin II, the protein sticks to another protein, called transducin. Before bumping into metarhodopsin II, transducin had tightly bound a small molecule called GDP. But when transducin interacts with metarhodopsin II, the GDP falls off, and a molecule called GTP binds to transducin. (GTP is closely related to, but different from, GDP.)

GTP-transducin-metarhodopsin II now binds to a protein called phosphodiesterase, located in the inner membrane of the cell. When attached to metarhodopsin II and its entourage, the phosphodiesterase acquires the chemical ability to "cut" a molecule called cGMP (a chemical relative of both GDP and GTP). Initially there are a lot of cGMP molecules in the cell, but the phosphodiesterase lowers its concentration, just as a pulled plug lowers the water level in a bathtub.

A transparent layer is also far more difficult to obtain than the researchers think. The best explanation for

5. M.J. Behe, *Darwin's Black Box: The Biochemical Challenge to Evolution* (New York, NY: The Free Press, 1996), p. 46.

the cornea's transparency is diffraction theory, which shows that light is not scattered if the refractive index doesn't vary over distances more than half the wavelength of light. This in turn requires a certain very finely organized structure of the corneal fibers, which in turn requires complicated chemical pumps to make sure there is exactly the right water content.[6]

Therefore, these simulations do not start from simple beginnings but presuppose vast complexity even to begin with. Also, in their original paper, the researchers admitted "an eye makes little sense on its own," because the ability to perceive light is meaningless unless the organism has sophisticated computational machinery to make use of this information. For example, it must have the ability to translate "attenuation of photon intensity" to "a shadow of a predator is responsible" to "I must take evasive measures," and be able to act on this information for it to have any selective value. Similarly, the first curving, with its slight ability to detect the direction of light, would only work if the creature had the appropriate "software" to interpret this. Perceiving actual images is more complicated still. And having the right hardware and software may not be enough — people who have their sight restored after years of blindness take some time to learn to see properly. It should be noted that much information processing occurs in the retina before the signal reaches the brain.

It is also fallacious to point to a series of more complex eyes in nature, and then argue that this presents an evolutionary sequence. This is like arranging a number of different types of aircraft in order of complexity, then claiming that the simple aircraft evolved into complex ones, as opposed to being designed. For one thing, eyes

---

6. P.W.V. Gurney, "Dawkins's Eye Revisited," *TJ* 15(3):92–99, 2001.

can't descend from other eyes *per se*; rather, organisms pass on genes for eyes to their descendants. This is important when considering the nautilus eye, a pinhole camera. This cannot possibly be an ancestor of the vertebrate lens/camera eye, because the nautilus as a whole is not an ancestor of the vertebrates, even according to the evolutionists!

ROTARY MOTORS IN THE BACTERIAL FLAGELLUM

Scientific American cites another difficult example of irreducible complexity — the rotary motors on bacterial flagellum, but it really has no answers.

15. RECENT DISCOVERIES PROVE THAT EVEN AT THE MICROSCOPIC LEVEL LIFE HAS A QUALITY OF COMPLEXITY THAT COULD NOT HAVE COME ABOUT THROUGH EVOLUTION.

"Irreducible complexity" is the battle cry of Michael J. Behe of Lehigh University, author of *Darwin's Black Box: The Biochemical Challenge to Evolution*. As a household example of irreducible complexity, Behe chooses the mousetrap — a machine that could not function if any of its pieces were missing and whose pieces have no value except as parts of the whole.

What is true of the mousetrap, he says, is even truer of the bacterial flagellum, a whiplike cellular organelle used for propulsion that operates like an outboard motor. The proteins that make up a flagellum are uncannily arranged into motor components, a universal joint, and other structures like those that a human engineer might specify. The possibility that this intricate array

could have arisen through evolutionary modification is virtually nil, Behe argues, and that be-
speaks intelligent design. [*SA* 84]

Indeed, it does (see diagram below).
He makes similar points about the blood's clotting
mechanism and other molecular systems.

> Yet evolutionary biologists have answers to
> these objections. First, there exist flagellae with
> forms simpler than the one that Behe cites, so it
> is not necessary for all those components to be
> present for a flagellum to work. The sophisticated
> components of this flagellum all have precedents

Bacterial flagellum with rotary motor, with the following features:
- Self assembly and repair
- Water-cooled rotary engine
- Proton motive force drive system
- Forward and reverse gears
- Operating speeds of up to 100,000 rpm
- Direction reversing capability within 1/4 of a turn
- Hard-wired signal transduction system with short-term
    memory.

(from Bacterial Flagella: *Paradigm for Design*, video,
<http://www.arn.org/arnproducts/videos/v021.htm>)

elsewhere in nature, as described by Kenneth R. Miller of Brown University and others. [*SA* 84]

Miller is hardly the epitome of reliability. Behe has also responded to critics such as Miller.[7]

In fact, the entire flagellum assembly is extremely similar to an organelle that *Yersinia pestis,* the bubonic plague bacterium, uses to inject toxins into cells. [*SA* 84]

This actually comes from the National Center for Science Education's misuses of the research of Dr. Scott Minnich, a geneticist and associate professor of microbiology at the University of Idaho. He is a world-class expert on the flagellum who says that belief in design has given him many research insights. His research shows that the flagellum won't form above 37°C, and instead some secretory organelles form from the same set of genes. But this secretory apparatus, as well as the plague bacterium's drilling apparatus, are a *degeneration* from the flagellum, which Minnich says came first although it is more complex.[8]

The key is that the flagellum's component structures, which Behe suggests have no value apart from their role in propulsion, can serve multiple functions that would have helped favor their evolution. [*SA* 84]

Actually, what Behe says he means by irreducible complexity is that the flagellum could not work without about 40 protein components all organized in the right way. *Scientific American*'s argument is like claiming that

---

7. Behe responds to various critics <http://www.trueorigin.org/behe08.asp>.
8. See Scott Minnich, "Bacterial Flagella: Spinning Tails of Complexity and Co-Option," <www.idurc.org/yale-minnich.html>.

if the components of an electric motor already exist in an electrical shop, they could assemble by themselves into a working motor. However, the right organization is just as important as the right components.

> The final evolution of the flagellum might then have involved only the novel recombination of sophisticated parts that initially evolved for other purposes. [*SA* 84]

Minnich points out that only about 10 of the 40 components can be explained by co-option, but the other 30 are brand new. Also, the very process of assembly *in the right sequence* requires other regulatory machines, so is in itself irreducibly complex.[9]

BLOOD CLOTTING

Scientific American cites another serious problem for evolution — blood clotting.

> Similarly, the blood-clotting system seems to involve the modification and elaboration of proteins that were originally used in digestion, according to studies by Russell F. Doolittle of the University of California at San Diego. So some of the complexity that Behe calls proof of intelligent design is not irreducible at all. [*SA* 84]

This is once more a lot of bluff by the atheist Doolittle, or at least poor reading comprehension. He cited recent experiments showing that mice could survive with two of the components of the blood clotting cascade (plasminogen and fibrinogen) eliminated. This supposedly showed that the current cascade was not irreducibly complex but clearly *reducibly* complex. But the

---

9. *Unlocking the Mysteries of Life*, video, Illustra Media, 2002.

experiment *really* showed that the mice lacking both components were better off than one lacking only plasminogen, because the latter suffer from uncleared clots. But the former are hardly as healthy as Doolittle implied, because the only reason they don't suffer from uncleared clots is that they have no functional clotting system at all! A non-functioning clotting system (despite possessing all the many remaining components) is hardly an evolutionary intermediate that natural selection could refine to produce a proper clotting system. Rather, this experiment is evidence against this, because the next step (i.e., from lacking both plasminogen and fibrinogen to fibrinogen only) would be selected *against* because of the uncleared clots.[10]

Complexity of a different kind — "specified complexity" — is the cornerstone of the intelligent-design arguments of William A. Dembski of Baylor University in his books *The Design Inference* and *No Free Lunch*. Essentially, his argument is that living things are complex in a way that undirected, random processes could never produce. The only logical conclusion, Dembski asserts, in an echo of Paley 200 years ago, is that some superhuman intelligence created and shaped life.

Dembski's argument contains several holes. It is wrong to insinuate that the field of explanations consists only of random processes or designing intelligences. Researchers into nonlinear systems and cellular automata at the Santa Fe Institute and elsewhere have demonstrated that simple, undirected processes can yield extraordinarily

10. For more information, see Behe's "In Defense of the Irreducibility of the Blood Clotting Cascade," <www.trueorigin.org/behe03.asp>.

complex patterns. Some of the complexity seen in organisms may therefore emerge through natural phenomena that we as yet barely understand. But that is far different from saying that the complexity could not have arisen naturally. [*SA* 84]

Talk about blind faith! But in practice, as Dembski points out, specified complexity in all cases but biology is used as evidence of design, including the search for extraterrestrial intelligence. Since biological complexity is the only exception proposed by evolutionists, it smacks of special pleading.[11]

In addition to the human eye, the flagellum, and blood clotting, there's a host of other examples of irreducible complexity in nature. Earlier I alluded to the dynamic sticking mechanism in the legs of insects. The sticky feet of geckos is another clear example of God's ingenuity.[12] Its structure is described by its evolutionary discoverers as "beyond the limits of human technology."[13] Still other examples of design include the lobster eyes with their unique square reflecting geometry that inspired advanced x-ray telescopes and beam producers,[14] the ATP synthase motor.

11. Russell Grigg, "A Brief History of Design," *Creation* 22(2):50–53 (March–May 2000).
12. J. Sarfati, "Great Gecko Glue?" *Creation* 23(1):54–55 (December 2000–February 2001).
13. K. Autumn et al., "Adhesive Force of a Single Gecko Foot Hair," *Nature* 405(6787): 681–685 (June 8, 2000); perspective by H. Gee, "Gripping Feat," same issue, p. 631.
14. J. Sarfati, "Lobster Eyes — Brilliant Geometric Design," *Creation* 23(3)12–13 (June–August 2001).

CHAPTER 11

ARGUMENT:
EVOLUTION OF SEX

Evolutionists say, "One of the so-called 'problems' of evolution — sexuality — can easily be explained."

PBS 5 was one of the most revealing about the conflicts between evolution and Christianity. The title is "Why Sex?" The usual propaganda is that "science" (stipulatively defined as evolution) is about facts/evidence or "how" questions, while religion deals with values/faith/morals or "why" questions. As explained in chapter 2, this is a faulty distinction, and this episode demonstrates this. Here, evolutionary psychology directly affects questions of sexual morality.

The program also spends much time discussing the *advantages* of a fully functional sexual reproductive system, but misleadingly implies that this is sufficient to explain its *origin*.

Sex is said to be more important than life itself, since it enables genes to be passed on to succeeding generations. PBS quotes extensively from Rutgers University evolutionary geneticist Robert Vrijenhoek, who said about sexual reproduction:

That's our immortality. That's what connects us to humans on into the future. That's what's connected us to all our ancestors in the past. That's what connects us to the ancestors that were fish, the ancestors that were protozoans, and the ancestors that were bacteria. [PBS 5]

Of course the series merely asserted this connection, apart from dubious implications from some common features (see chapter 6). It's also important to note how evolution directly impinges on "religion" despite the claims that they are compatible (see chapter 2). Vrijenhoek implies that immortality has nothing to do with survival of the individual.

ASEXUAL V. SEXUAL REPRODUCTION

The PBS 5 takes its cameras to Texas, where scientists investigated lizards that were entirely female. They laid eggs that hatched into lizards that were clones of the mother. This is called parthenogenesis, from Greek *parthenos* (virgin) and Latin *genesis* (from Greek *gignesthai* [to be born]). They seemed to do very well, so what's the point of sex?

Disadvantages of sexual reproduction

Indeed, the program acknowledges that sex has many disadvantages, e.g., only 50 percent of the genes are passed on to an offspring. This means that there is a 50 percent chance of losing a beneficial mutation. And in a stable population (i.e., not changing the number of individuals), there is on average one surviving offspring per parent, so asexual reproduction is twice as efficient at passing on genes to the next generation. Sex also means that an optimal gene configuration can never be passed on in its entirety.

It is also biologically costly to maintain the sex organs, and to maintain mechanisms to stop the male's immune system destroying his own (genetically different) sperm, and stop the female's immune system destroying incoming sperm or the offspring she carries (in viviparous organisms). And as will be seen in the sexual selection section below, sometimes sexual displays can be cumbersome and make the organism more vulnerable. Females obviously expend a lot of time and energy if they must bear live young. It takes energy to find a mate, otherwise the organism will die without passing on its genes, and if one sex is eliminated, the species will become extinct. It's a lot of trouble, considering that asexual organisms such as bacteria reproduce very quickly.

Because of these lizards, the narrator posed the question, "Are males really necessary?" Males eat about half the food, and it means that only half the members of the population (females) are involved directly in bearing young. In an asexual population, *all* its members bear offspring directly.

Advantages of sexual reproduction

Since sexually reproducing species do well, males must have their uses. PBS 5 then shifts to a pool in Sonora, Mexico, inhabited by a species of minnows, both asexually and sexually reproducing ones. But they are infested with a parasite that causes black spot disease. PBS again quotes geneticist Vrijenhoek, who says that the sexually reproducing minnows are more resistant than the asexual ones.

The researchers invoked the "Red Queen Hypothesis," invented by Lee van Valen; Alice (in Wonderland) raced the Red Queen, and exclaimed that they had to keep running just to stay in the same relative position. Evolution is supposed to be a race, and the asexual minnows produced clones, then stopped evolving, so are easy targets. But the sexually reproducing minnows produced lots of variation, so presented a *moving* target. But other evolutionists say, "The Red Queen idea is simply a cute name for a zoological myth."[1]

This neat hypothesis seemed to be questioned when a drought eliminated the minnows. When the pool was naturally recolonized, the parasites killed the sexually reproducing ones faster. But it turned out that human-introduced sexually reproducing minnows were still the most resistant of all. The natural colonizers turned out to be inbred, so lost the advantage of variability.

So it seems that the variability is a major advantage, and well worth paying the price of transmitting only 50 percent of the genes, and the other disadvantages of males. Sexual reproduction also has a 50 percent chance of losing a harmful mutation without cost to the population (death of an individual).

Advantage doesn't explain origin!

Creationists can explain the origin of fully functioning sexual reproduction, from the start, in an optimal and genetically diverse population. Once the mechanisms *are already in place*, they have these advantages. But simply having advantages doesn't remotely explain how they could be built from scratch. The hypothetical transitional forms would be highly disadvantageous, so natural selection would work *against* them. In many cases, the male and female genitalia are precisely tuned so one could fit the other, meaning that they could not have evolved independently.

EVOLUTION OF SEX?

PBS 5 features a cute cartoon of two single-celled creatures with eyes, kissing and exchanging genes. Then the narrator intones:

---

1. L. Margulis and D. Sagan, *What Is Sex?* (New York, NY: Simon and Schuster, 1997), p. 121.

Random change produced a creature that was small and fast, which turned out to be an evolutionary advantage. Organisms with reproductive cells like that are called males. Their goal is to find organisms with a different speciality — providing the nutrients life requires. They're called females. These early pioneers evolved into sperm and eggs. [PBS 5]

Hang on — not only is slick animation no substitute for evidence, but somewhere along the line this program jumped from alleged male and female single-celled creatures to multicellular organisms *containing* cells like them. The narrator continued:

Males produce sperm by the millions — with so many potential offspring, it doesn't pay to be fussy about eggs. A better strategy is to try to fertilize as many eggs as you can. Eggs are more complex than sperm and take a larger investment of energy. Females make a limited number of them. Fewer eggs mean fewer chances to pass on genes, and that means that females — unlike males — do better if they're choosy. At a deep biological level, males and females want different things, regardless of how things appear on the surface. . . . Small sperm versus large eggs. . . . Quantity versus quality. [PBS 5]

At about the same time, the program showed a man and woman under a sheet, probably naked but not showing too much of that, indulging in sexual foreplay, then lots of sequences of animals having sex. Is this program really meant for young schoolchildren?

Then the program explains male competition for mates and ornate sexual displays, while females exercise choice. Supposedly the concept of female choice was often discounted in Victorian England (with a female head of state who ruled for more than 60 years).

But the program shifts to a role-reversing bird in Panama. Supposedly, the crocodiles eat so many chicks that females leave the males in charge of the eggs while they try to reproduce again. The females are the ones that keep harems, and kill chicks and break eggs of other females. The narrator says:

> So now it's the females who care more about quality than quantity. Now it's the females who fight over mates. Over time, they take on traditionally male characteristics. . . . So here is an evolutionary revelation about gender. Male and female roles are not set in stone. They're largely determined by which sex competes for mates, and which invests in the young. [PBS 5]

But before, it was the relative size and speed of sperm and egg that caused males to compete and females to invest more time with their offspring, and other behavioral differences. Now, competition and investment in young are no longer *effects* but are themselves *causes* that overturn the roles expected from the differences in gametes. What this really means is that evolution as an explanatory framework is so plastic that its proponents can explain mutually contradictory states of affairs, if they have enough imagination to create plausible just-so stories.

In line with the rest of the series, PBS 5 aims to indoctrinate readers to think that the origin of sex is well explained by evolution. A decent documentary would not have censored evidence against this view. In reality, evolutionists really have no idea how sex could have evolved. Even the atheist Richard Dawkins says:

To say, as I have, that good genes can benefit from the existence of sex whereas bad genes can benefit from its absence, is not the same thing as explaining why sex is there at all. There are many theories of why sex exists, and none of them is knock-down convincing. . . . Maybe one day I'll summon up the courage to tackle it in full and write a whole book on the origin of sex.[2]

The smug assurances of the PBS program are also contradicted by the evolutionist journal *Science*: "How sex began and why it thrived remain a mystery."[3]

SEXUAL SELECTION

Darwin is most famous for the idea that natural selection is a driving force behind evolution. But he realized that this would not explain a number of features that seem to be a hindrance, e.g., the peacock tail. So Darwin invoked the idea of sexual selection, where choice by the opposite sex played a huge part in determining which individuals were able to pass on their genes. Later on, sexual selection is invoked to explain the human brain.

Creationists deny neither natural nor sexual selection. For example, we think it's likely that sexual selection augmented natural selection in producing the different people groups ("races") from a single population of humans that were isolated after Babel.[4]

The difference is that creationists recognize that selection can work only on *existing* genetic information.

2. R. Dawkins, *Climbing Mt. Improbable* (Harmondsworth, Middlesex, England: Penguin Books Ltd., 1997), p. 75.
3. B. Wuethrich, "Why Sex? Putting the Theory to the Test," *Science* 281:1980–1982, 1998.
4. The human "races" issue is covered more fully in K. Ham, C. Wieland, and D. Batten, *One Blood — The Biblical Answer to Racism* (Green Forest, AR: Master Books, Inc., 2000).

Evolutionists believe that mutation provides *new* information for selection. But no known mutation has ever increased genetic information, although there should be many examples observable today if mutation/selection were truly adequate to explain the goo-to-you theory.[5]

CHIMPS AND BONOBOS

The common chimpanzee *Pan troglodytes* and the bonobo (or pygmy chimp) *Pan paniscus* hybridize, so are the same biblical kind. Sometimes they are classified as the subspecies *Pan troglodytes troglodytes* and *P. t. paniscus,* respectively, within the same species. Although they look similar, live in similar environments, and eat similar food, their behavior is different.

Chimps are violent, and bonobos are peaceful. PBS 5 program shows the San Diego Wild Animal Park, and displays bonobos having "every imaginable" type of recreational copulation, both heterosexual and homosexual, with a running commentary worthy of a hyper-testosteronic adolescent schoolboy.

So how is their behavior explained? Supposedly by female solidarity: they "can form alliances and cooperatively dominate males" whereas the chimp males abuse females. So how to explain female solidarity? "A relatively simple change in feeding ecology was responsible for this dramatic difference in social behavior." Female bonobos forage on the ground, so have opportunities for social interaction. Female chimps can't do this because gorillas eat the food on the ground, so females must forage on fruit trees alone. Supposedly a drought two million years ago killed the gorillas, and enabled a population of chimps

---

5. Note that even if such a mutation were ever discovered, evolutionists would still need to find hundreds more to give their theory the observational boost it desperately needs. See L. Spetner, *Not by Chance* (New York, NY: Judaica Press, 1999); also see Carl Wieland, AiG's views on the intelligent design movement, <www.answersingenesis.org/IDM>, August 30, 2002.

to forage on the ground and evolve into bonobos. What a pity, says the program, that we didn't have a similar history and evolve "to be a totally different, more peaceful, less violent, and more sexual species."

As usual, we shouldn't expect actual *evidence* for this story. From the available evidence, it's impossible to prove cause-effect. In other words, how can we disprove that it was the other way round, i.e., that female solidarity didn't generate ground foraging behavior, or even that a gorilla invasion didn't cause bonobos to devolve into chimps?

SEXUAL MORALITY V. EVOLUTIONARY PSYCHOLOGY

A female may well want the male with the best genes to ensure that her offspring are the "fittest." But her best strategy for offspring survival could be finding a male who will stick around and help her care for the young. The male's best strategy is to make sure the offspring are his, so monogamy would have a selective advantage.

But other evolutionary forces threaten monogamy. For example, songbirds are monogamous, but sometimes a female will lust after a male with stronger genes. But this is risky — if the "husband" finds out, he could kill the offspring.

Concepts from animals are applied to humans in the new field of evolutionary psychology. In the PBS program, Geoffrey Miller claimed that our brain is too extravagant to have evolved by natural selection. He claimed, "It wasn't God, it was our ancestors," via sexual selection, that shaped our brain "by choosing their sexual partners for their brains, for their behavior, during courtship." Art, music, and humor played the part of the peacock tail.

Supposedly this is borne out by tests of human attraction. Men prefer women's faces with full lips, indicating high estrogen; and other facial features, indicating low testosterone. Both are indicators of fertility. So now males do make choices despite having fast and small sperm? Once more, evolution explains *any* state of affairs, so really explains nothing.

Women looking for a short-term fling, or who are ovulating, prefer more masculine faces, indicating "good" genes. But they prefer more feminine "gentler" men for a long-term relationship, because they will be more likely to help care for her children. But appearances can be deceptive. We also wonder whether a face of a person from a different people group would be picked as often, although there is no disadvantage to the offspring's genes from so-called inter-racial marriages.[6]

While there's a fleeting disclaimer that evolutionary psychology is controversial even among evolutionists, this program presents Miller's ideas uncritically and unchallenged. But a review of his book, *The Mating Mind,* in *New Scientist* said:

> How does one actually test these ideas? Without a concerted effort to do this, evolutionary psychology will remain in the realms of armchair entertainment rather than real science.[7]

A leading evolutionary paleoanthropologist, Ian Tattersall, was equally scathing of Miller's book:

> In the end we are looking here at the product of a storyteller's art, not of science.[8]

---

6. K. Ham, "Inter-racial Marriage: Is It Biblical?" *Creation* 21(3):22–25 (June–August 1999).
7. T. Birkhead, "Strictly for the Birds," review of *The Mating Mind* by Geoffrey Miller, *New Scientist,* p. 48–49 (May 13, 2000).
8. I. Tattersall, "Whatever Turns You On." review of *The Mating Mind* by Geoffrey Miller, *New York Times Book Review* (June 11, 2000).

WHY AN EPISODE ON SEX?

In searching for explanations as to why evolutionists would feel passionately enough about their belief system to spend so many millions foisting it upon the public as in the PBS *Evolution* series, one may not have to look much further than this segment. It is as if those looking for justification of an "anything goes" approach to sexual morality have had a major hand in this segment. With humans already portrayed as just an advanced species of ape, and sex as a mere tool for propagation of genes, the way the program dwelt on the random hetero/homo "flings" of our alleged bonobo "cousins," and the association with an allegedly superior, more peaceful lifestyle, was telling.

CHAPTER 12

ARGUMENT: EVOLUTION OF MANKIND

Evolutionists say, "The unique characteristics of the human species can easily be explained."

PBS 6 — "The Mind's Big Bang" — attempts to explain the biggest difference between humans and animals: our mind, including the advantages of language. However, it makes hardly any attempt to *prove* evolution; rather, it *assumes* it, and makes up stories to explain the differences given this assumption. PBS 1 had already paved the way with misleading arguments about ape-men and DNA similarity.

HAVE HUMANS EVOLVED FROM APE-LIKE CREATURES?

The similarity between apes and humans is one of evolutionists' favorite arguments for common descent based on common appearance. The PBS series shouts "yes" in answer to the question, "Have humans evolved from ape-like creatures?" and episode 1 showed a number of fossils of alleged "ape-men" for cumulative effect. But this was very deceptive — some of the alleged "ape-men" it showed are not even accepted by evolutionists as genuine intermediates anymore. For example, it showed an old photograph of Louis Leakey with *Zinjanthropus* (now *Paranthropus*) *boisei* or "Nutcracker Man," sometimes called a robust australopithecine. But this was long ago relegated to a side branch on man's alleged evolutionary tree.

PBS 1 also claimed that the DNA of chimps and humans was "98 percent" similar, and said it's "only a couple of spelling errors." While the 98 percent is debatable,[1] claiming a "couple" of differences is outright deception — humans have 3 billion "letters" (base pairs) of DNA information in each cell, so a two percent difference is actually 60 million "spelling errors"! Of course, this is not "error" but twenty 500-page books worth of new information that needs to be explained by mutation and selection. Even if we grant 10 million years to the evolutionists, population genetics studies show that animals with human-like generation times of about 20 years could accumulate only about 1,700 mutations — not 60 million — in their genomes in that time frame.[2]

MISSING LINKS FOUND?

Donald Johanson, the discoverer of the alleged missing link "Lucy," was featured on PBS 2 titled "Great Transformations." Supposedly, humans are part of evolution, despite our unique abilities to design and create works of art. Allegedly, about 7 million years ago, our ancestors swung down from the trees and became bipedal. Then they could gather and carry food, and this food could be higher in energy. This fed bigger brains, which in turn helped food to be gathered more efficiently, in a

---

1. See also Don Batten, "Human/chimp DNA Similarity: Evidence for Evolutionary Relationship?" *Creation* 19(1):21–22 (December 1996–February 1997).
2. W.J. ReMine, The Biotic Message (St. Paul, MN: St. Paul Science, 1993), chapter 8.

positive feedback. But Johanson said that there are still differences in the skeletons of chimps and humans, e.g., differently shaped pelvises, different angles where the spine meets the skull, and the way we walk with our knees together while apes walk with their legs far apart.

But PBS offered little actual evidence. The fossil record is full of holes, and "missing link" claims become boring after a while because they are so often discredited.[3] The nearest thing to "evidence" was Liza Shapiro, University of Texas, showing how flexible the lemur's spine was. The lemur can move on all fours, but leap upright. But this doesn't show how a quadruped can make all the transformations needed to turn it into a proper biped.

Scientific American also asserts that we have found a series of hominid fossils that link humans to an ape-like ancestor:

> The historical nature of macroevolutionary study involves inference from fossils and DNA rather than direct observation. . . . For instance, evolution implies that between the earliest-known ancestors of humans (roughly five million years old) and the appearance of anatomically modern humans (about 100,000 years ago), one should find a succession of hominid creatures with features progressively less ape-like and more modern, which is indeed what the fossil record shows. [*SA* 80]

Scientific American also makes this amazing claim:

> Perhaps 20 or more hominids (not all of them our ancestors) fill the gap between Lucy the australopithecine and modern humans. [*SA* 83]

---

3. For example, see J. Sarfati, *"Time's* Alleged 'Ape-man' Trips Up (Again)," *TJ* 15(3) 2001.

How could these alleged "20 or more hominids" fill the gap if they are "not all our ancestors"? That is, they have fallen out of the gap and into a side alley.

The **Power** of **Presuppositions...**

Three different interpretations of what the fossil *Australopithecus boisei* looked like from the same skull remains.

This shows the imagination of scientists and artists. Such "reconstructions" can be made ape-like or human, depending on the artist's viewpoint or belief system.

The "links" are still missing!

The "ape-men" fossils are often based on fragmentary remains, and this is true of the latest of a long series of "missing link claims," *Ardipithecus ramidus kadabba*. But when more bones are excavated, the specimens are found to be either man or non-man (e.g., australopithecine).

Even if there were such a chain of similar creatures, common appearance does *not* prove common origin. But the claim is groundless, anyway. What the fossil record shows in reality, even granted the evolutionary "dating" methods, is that this alleged clear-cut progression exists only in the minds of evolutionary popularists. Marvin Lubenow shows that the various alleged "ape-men" do not form a smooth sequence in evolutionary "ages," but overlap considerably.[4] For example, the time-span of *Homo sapiens* fossils contains the time-span of the fossils of *Homo erectus,* supposedly our ancestor. Also, when the various fossils are analyzed in depth, they turn out not to be transitional or even mosaic. The morphology

4. M. Lubenow, *Bones of Contention* (Grand Rapids, MI: Baker Books, 1992).

overlaps too — the analysis of a number of characteristics indicates that *Homo ergaster, H. erectus, H. neanderthalensis* as well as *H. heidelbergensis*, were most likely "racial" variants of modern man, while *H. habilis* and another specimen called *H. rudolfensis* were just types of australopithecines.[5] In fact, *H. habilis* is now regarded as an invalid name, probably caused by assigning fragments of australopithecines and *H. erectus* fossils into this "taxonomic waste bin."

OUT OF AFRICA?

PBS 6 begins deep in a cave in France, where archaeologist Randy White explores cave paintings, allegedly 30–40 ka (kilo-annum = thousand years ago). The narrator intones about finding out how our ancestors became truly human, and how the mind was born. Then the scene shifts to the Rift Valley in East Africa, where "humans began."

Supposedly our branch of the evolutionary tree split off 6 Ma (mega-annum = million years ago) from the line leading to chimps. Our ancestors swung down from the trees and became bipedal about 4 Ma, tools were first made 2.5 Ma, early humans began to leave Africa 2 Ma but they would all eventually become extinct, while truly modern humans left Africa 50–60 ka. This is all "documented" with computer graphics, then by actors.

Internal evolutionary squabbles overlooked

As shown later, PBS 6 advocates what is called the "out of Africa" model, without saying so. This is where modern humans came out of Africa and replaced less evolved hominids that had emerged from Africa much earlier. But there is another evolutionary idea, called the

5. J. Woodmorappe, "The Non-transitions in 'Human Evolution' — on Evolutionists' Terms," *TJ* 13(2):10–13, 1999.

"multi-regional" or "regional-continuity" hypothesis, where the hominids that emerged from Africa 2 Ma evolved into modern humans in many parts of the world. This is one of the most vitriolic debates among paleo-anthropologists, yet this episode presents only one side. The acrimony between the proponents of these rival theories is due, according to anthropologist Peter Underhill of Stanford University, to: "Egos, egos, egos. Scientists are human." We think *both* sides are right — in their criticisms of each other, because humans did not evolve at all![6]

Human distinctives

PBS 6 showed a skull "dated" 100 ka, and said that the owner could have been dressed in modern clothes and it would hardly raise an eyebrow. Massachusetts Institute of Technology psychologist Steven Pinker pointed out that modern human babies anywhere in the world can learn any language in the world, and how to count, as well as grow to understand computers. So he suggested: "The distinctively human parts of our intelligence were in place before our ancestors split off into the different continents."

The humans who allegedly left Africa 50–60 ka encountered the hominids that had left earlier, that had evolved into Neandertals. They were bigger and stronger than we are, had bigger brains, and were characterized by having a big nose, receding chin (prognathism) and forehead, almost no cheek, and prominent brow ridges (supraorbital tori). But they were less creative, with almost no symbolic life or art, and unstructured burial of their dead. Their spear tips were easy to make by chipping stone,

6. For an explanation of both the "out of Africa" and "regional-continuity" ideas and a biblical alternative, see C. Wieland, "No Bones about Eve," *Creation* 13(4):20–23 (September–November 1991); <www.answersingenesis.org/eve2>.

but had low range so were used mainly for stabbing. Supposedly they learned by imitation, rather than passing on information via a highly developed language.

The late arrivals, however, had a structured burial of their dead, and made long-range spears with some difficulty by carving antlers for tips. They also invented a spear thrower. Most importantly, they had a sophisticated language that enabled them to transmit information across both distance and time.

They also produced art and culture. PBS 6 demonstrates a "spit painting" technique they could have used for their cave paintings, and shows that they may have played music by using speleothems (stalactites and stalagmites) as natural percussion instruments.

CREATIONIST VIEW OF CAVE MEN AND NEANDERTALS

The Bible teaches that the first man, Adam, was made from dust and the first woman was made from his rib. Also, Genesis 1 teaches that living creatures reproduce "after their kind" — see chapter 4. Therefore, we would expect no continuity between man and the animals.

Cave men and the Bible

One important event recorded in the Bible is the confusion of languages at Babel. The obvious effect was to produce the major language families, from which modern languages have developed. But the division of people according to their newly created language groups had other effects, too.

Babel resulted in the isolation of small people groups, each containing a fraction of the total gene pool. This would help fix certain characteristics. Natural selection and sexual selection would act on these, producing the different people groups ("races") we see today.

Also, some people groups would be isolated from civilization. Consider even the typical small extended family group today, if suddenly isolated from civilization, e.g., on a desert island. Many such groups would not have the ability to smelt metals or build houses. Therefore, they would have to use the hardest material available (stone) and make use of already-existing structures (caves). Different family groups would also have different levels of artistic ability. So it shouldn't be too difficult to accept that humans such as *Homo erectus* and Neandertals were probably post-Babel humans who became isolated from major cities, and developed certain physical characteristics because certain genes became fixed due to the small population and selective factors. The notion of a "stone age" is fallacious — rather, it's a cave/stone technology stage of different people groups. Some people even today have this level of technology, but they live at the same time as us, and are just as human.

HUMAN BRAIN UNIQUENESS

PBS 6 quotes the psychologist Pinker again, who points out that the human brain contains 100 billion cells, and more importantly, it is wired with 100 trillion connections, "wiring it in precise ways to produce intelligence." But he attributed this to mutations over 10s and 100s of thousands of years. He has yet to find a single mutation that could increase information, let alone the colossal number required to wire the cerebral supercomputer correctly.

Supposedly, this would have been driven by selection for ability to manipulate others. Better language control means better social control.

Human v. chimp minds

The PBS episode turns to psychologist Andrew Whiten of the University of St. Andrews in Scotland, who tested how young children learned. (Incidentally, on the lintel above the entryway to the school is the Latin "*In principio erat Verbum*," the Vulgate translation of John 1:1, "In the beginning was the Word.") He tested children with small models of people, where one "person" puts an object in one place, goes away, then another "person" takes this object and hides it somewhere else. Then the first "person" returns, whereupon the child is asked where he or she would look for the object. A three year old suggests the new hiding place, while a five year old correctly realizes that the first "person" would have no way of knowing that the object had been moved, and would look in the place he left it. (Sometimes this is called the "Sally-Anne" test, where the "Sally" doll hides something in the absence of "Anne.") Whiten concluded that by the age of three:

> A child cannot ascribe actions to others. But by the age of five, the child's brain has developed the capacity for stepping into someone else's mind. [PBS 6]

The program contrasts this with chimpanzees, which are incapable of this at any age, "No chimp has passed the test of attribution of false belief."

Language

There are about 6,300 languages in the world today. They all have certain constraints, and obey strict rules, called syntax. This enables us to hierarchically organize information, which is something chimps cannot do, even with the best training in signing.

There is a certain window of opportunity for learning syntax by imitation that gradually closes after the age of seven. PBS 6 shifted to Managua, the capital of Nicaragua, where we meet "Mary No-name." She was born deaf, and no one taught her sign language, so she never had a chance to learn syntax. She is still intelligent enough to communicate with some signs, but only to people who know the context.

PBS 6 documents how after the Nicaraguan revolution, U.S. sign language experts tried to teach sign language to deaf people from isolated villages, but failed. But the children developed their own sign language instead, which is a real language with proper syntax and as much capacity for expressing complex thought as spoken language. They wanted to communicate with other people like themselves rather than have a language imposed upon them.

Deaf people actually process sign language with the same areas of the brain that hearing people use to process spoken language, including Broca's area and Wernicke's area. This is shown by deaf patients who have damage to either area, who have an equivalent type of aphasia (language impairment) in sign language to that which a hearing person would suffer in spoken language.[7]

Evolution of language?

None of the above has anything to do with evolution. The language processing areas are unique to humans, and enable us to use syntax in both written and sign language.

All the same, atheist Richard Dawkins of Oxford University presents his usual storytelling on PBS 6 about how language conferred a selective advantage, so left more offspring. It's interesting that the only topic this well-known propagandist for neo-Darwinism is interviewed on is language, although Dawkins's field is biology, not linguistics. It's also notable that the PBS series

---

7. G. Hickok, U. Bellugi, and E.S. Klima, "Sign Language in the Brain," *Scientific American* 284(6):42–49 (June 2001).

did not show Dawkins promoting his rabid atheistic religion, which he makes plain is a main reason for his promotion of Darwin. Presumably the producers didn't want to make the materialistic implications of evolution *too* obvious to an American public that might still be repulsed by overt atheism.

PBS 6 explains how Robin Dunbar of Liverpool University has researched the way people use language, and he rejects the idea that the main function is to exchange information. Rather, about two-thirds is social interaction, which he called "gossip." So natural selection favored those with the most refined social skills, which would have the advantages of holding big groups together and being able to find out information about third parties.

Difficulties with language evolution

It's one thing to claim that languages evolved, but it's another to provide a mechanism. Evolutionists usually claim that languages evolved from animal grunts. Some even claim that the continuing change of languages is just like biological evolution. However, actual observations of language present a very different picture.

First, ancient languages were actually extremely complex with many different inflections. There is no hint of any build-up from simpler languages. For example, in the Indo-European family, Sanskrit, Classical Greek and Latin had many different noun inflections for different case, gender, and number, while verbs were inflected for tense, voice, number, and person. Modern descendants of these languages have greatly *reduced* the number of inflections, i.e., the trend is from complex to simpler, the *opposite* of evolution. English has almost completely lost inflections, retaining just a few like the possessive "s."

English has also lost 65–85 percent of the Old English vocabulary, and many Classical Latin words have also been lost from its descendants, the Romance languages (Spanish, French, Italian, etc.).

Second, most of the changes were *not* random, but the result of *intelligence*. For example: forming compound words by joining simple words and derivations, by adding prefixes and suffixes, by modification of meaning, and by borrowing words from other languages including calques (a borrowed compound word where each component is translated and then joined). There are also unconscious, but definitely non-random, changes such as systematic sound shifts, for example those described by Grimm's law (which relates many Germanic words to Latin and Greek words).[8]

MEMES

Dawkins said on PBS 6, "The Mind's Big Bang":

> The only kind of evolutionary change we're likely to see very much of is not genetic information at all, it's cultural evolution. And if we put a Darwinian spin on that, then we're going to be talking about the differential survival of memes, as opposed to genes. [PBS 6]

Dawkins proposed the meme idea long ago in his book *The Selfish Gene*, and psychologist Sue Blackmore of the University of West of England has been one of his recent champions. She said on PBS 6:

> Memes are ideas, habits, skills, gestures, stories, songs — anything which we pass from person to person by imitation. We copy them. . . .

8. K. May, "Talking Point," *Creation* 23(2):42–45 (March–May 2001), and A. Steel, "The Development of Languages Is Nothing Like Biological Evolution," *TJ* 14(2), 2000.

just as the competition between genes shapes all of biological evolution, so it's the competition between memes that shapes our minds and cultures.

Nowadays I would say that memetic evolution is going faster and faster, and it has almost entirely taken over from biological evolution. . . .

The more educated you are, the less children you have. That is memes fighting against genes. [PBS 6]

Now memes have apparently found a new home, the Internet, and it has actually enslaved us, we are told.

Blackmore even believes that the idea of the "self" is an illusion produced by competing memes in the brain. But under her own system, we must ask her, "Who is (or rather, what are) actually proposing this idea?"!

But it becomes ridiculous when things such as the Internet, birth control, any invention, insulin, are called "memes." A term that describes everything really describes nothing. All that she's done is apply the same label to just about anything, but this adds nothing to our knowledge.

It's no wonder that the evolutionist Jerry Coyne called Blackmore's book "a work not of science, but of extreme advocacy." He says that memes are "but a flashy new wrapping around a parcel of old and conventional ideas." Coyne also believes that evolutionary psychology is nonscience (and nonsense). Coyne is no creationist sympathizer but an ardent — but ineffective — opponent of creation.[9]

The Discovery Institute critique of the PBS series points out that, if the likes of Eugenie Scott were truly

9. See C. Wieland, "New Eyes for Blind Cave Fish?" <www.answersingenesis.org/cave_fish>.

concerned about non-science being taught in the science classroom, she would oppose evolutionary psychology and memetic evolution as well, and certainly not support the use of this PBS series in science classrooms.[10] No, what she's opposed to are challenges to her materialistic faith.

CONCLUSION

From all the money and time lavished on the PBS "Evolution" series, major articles in science journals, and political campaigns to keep teachers from presenting alternatives to evolution in schools, it is evident that the evolutionists fear the increasing spread of creationist information, despite their best efforts at censorship. So they are desperate to counteract this information. But their efforts don't withstand scientific scrutiny, and in the end any reasonable observer would have to admit that evolution is a deduction from a materialistic belief system. It is philosophy/religion dressed up as "science."

---

10. The Discovery Institute's critique makes these good points in *Getting the Facts Straight: A Viewer's Guide to PBS's Evolution* (Seattle, WA: Discovery Institute Press, 2001).

APPENDIXES

This book has been organized around the most powerful arguments that evolutionists can muster (quoting the salient points of **PBS** and *Scientific American*) against the best arguments of creationists. Too often, both sides get sidetracked on bad arguments. We believe that all Bible-believers should have solid answers about the real issues of the debate (e.g., two world views are in conflict; we disagree about interpretation, not the facts themselves).

This doesn't mean that Christians should ignore the weak arguments or the potshots. We have added an appendix to address some of these arguments.

APPENDIX 1: COMMON ARGUMENTS FOR EVOLUTION THAT HAVE BEEN REJECTED

REJECTED ARGUMENT 1: SIMILARITIES BETWEEN EMBRYOS[1]

Most people have heard that the human embryo goes through various evolutionary stages, such as having gill slits like a fish, a tail like a monkey, etc. This concept, pretentiously called the "biogenetic law," was popularized by the German evolutionist Ernst Haeckel in the late 1860s. It is also known as "embryonic recapitulation" or "ontogeny recapitulates phylogeny," meaning that during an organism's early development it supposedly re-traces its evolutionary history.

Although this idea was based on a fraud and has been debunked by many high-profile scientists, the idea persists.

---

1. Adapted with permission from chapter 7 of Ken Ham, Andrew Snelling, and Carl Wieland, *The Answers Book* (Green Forest, AR: Master Books, 1990).

Even textbooks in the 1990s were still using Haeckel's fraudulent drawings.[2]

Haeckel's fraud exposed

Within months of the publication of Haeckel's work in 1868, L. Rtimeyer, professor of zoology and comparative anatomy at the University of Basel, showed it to be fraudulent. William His Sr., professor of anatomy at the University of Leipzig, and a famous comparative embryologist, corroborated Rtimeyer's criticisms.[3] These scientists showed that Haeckel fraudulently modified his drawings of embryos to make them look more alike. Haeckel even reprinted some woodcuts and then claimed they were embryos of different species!

Has the "biogenetic law" any merit? In 1965, evolutionist George Gaylord Simpson said, "It is now firmly established that ontogeny does not repeat phylogeny."[4] Prof. Keith Thompson (biology, Yale) said:

> Surely the biogenetic law is as dead as a doornail. It was finally exorcised from biology textbooks in the fifties. As a topic of serious theoretical inquiry, it was extinct in the twenties.[5]

Despite the evidence of fraud, Haeckel's drawings are still widely believed to bear some resemblance to reality. But a recent investigation, published in 1997, has revealed that Haeckel's fraud was far worse than anyone realized. An embryologist, Dr. Michael

2. P.H. Raven and G.B. Johnson, *Biology* (3rd edition) (St. Louis, MO: Mosby–Year Book, 1992), p. 396. For example, S. Gilbert, *Developmental Biology* (5th edition) (MA: Sinauer Associates,, 1997), p. 254, 900. Gilbert wrongly credits the drawings to "Romanes, 1901."

3. W.H. Rusch Sr., "Ontogeny Recapitulates Phylogeny," *Creation Research Society Quarterly* 6 (1):27–34, 1969.

4. Simpson and Beck, *An Introduction to Biology*, p. 241, 1965.

5. K. Thompson, "Ontogeny and Phylogeny Recapitulated," *American Scientist* 76:273, 1988.

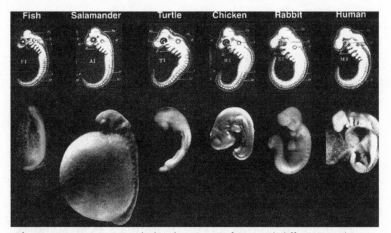

Above, top row: Haeckel's drawings of several different embryos, showing incredible similarity in their early "tailbud" stage.
Bottom row: Richardson's photographs of how the embryos *really* look at the same stage of development.

Richardson, with the co-operation of biologists around the world, collected and photographed the types of embryos Haeckel supposedly drew.[6] Dr. Richardson found that Haeckel's drawings bore little resemblance to the embryos.[7] *The Times* (London) quotes Richardson:

> This is one of the worst cases of scientific fraud. It's shocking to find that somebody one thought was a great scientist was deliberately misleading. It makes me angry. What he [Haeckel] did was to take a human embryo and copy it, pretending that the salamander and the pig and

6. The embryo photos used in this article were kindly supplied by Dr. Michael K. Richardson. They originally appeared in M.K. Richardson et al., © Springer-Verlag GmbH & Co., Tiergartenstrasse, 69121 Heidelberg, Germany, 1997. There is no highly conserved stage in the vertebrates: implications for current theories of evolution and development, *Anatomy and Embryology* 196(2):91–106.
7. R. Grigg, "Fraud Rediscovered," *Creation* 20(2):49–51, 1998; also Richardson et al., reference 6.

all the others looked the same at the same stage of development. They don't. These are fakes.[8]

A human embryo never looks reptilian or pig-like. A human embryo is always a human embryo, from the moment of conception; it is never anything else. It does not *become* human sometime after eight weeks. This is what the Bible says — the unborn baby is a tiny human child (Gen. 25:21–22, Ps. 139:13–16, Jer. 1:5, Luke 1:41–44).

Similarities in early embryos are inevitable

Admittedly, the embryos of animals bear some resemblance in their early stages of development. But this makes perfect sense from a design standpoint. To construct anything, you begin with something without shape, or with a basic form, and then you add increasingly specialized details.

An illustration from pottery may help. A potter starts with a lump of clay. Whether he wants to make a goblet or a slender vase, the potter shapes the clay initially into a cylinder. At this stage both the goblet and the vase look similar — they have the same basic plan. Further work results in the goblet and vase looking more and more different. (The analogy with embryos breaks down in that the potter could change his mind and make *either* a vase or goblet at the completion of the basic plan. A fish embryo, however, could never become a human embryo [or vice versa] because a fish embryo has the coded instructions only for making a fish.)

Some principles known as *von Baer's laws* express this concept in regard to embryo development. Namely, the general features of animals appear earlier in the

---

8. N. Hawkes, *The Times* (London), August 11, 1997, p. 14.

embryo's development than the specialized features. Each embryo of a given species, instead of passing through the stages of other animals, departs more and more from them as it develops.

Von Baer's laws indicate that the younger the embryonic stage, the more closely organisms tend to resemble each other.

REJECTED ARGUMENT 2: PEPPERED MOTHS

The "textbook story" of England's famous peppered moths (*Biston betularia*) goes like this. The moth comes in light and dark (melanic) forms. Pollution from the Industrial Revolution darkened the tree trunks, mostly by killing the light-colored covering lichen (plus soot).

The lighter forms, which had been well camouflaged against the light background, now "stood out," and so birds more readily ate them. Therefore, the proportion of dark moths increased dramatically. Later, as pollution was cleaned up, the light moth became predominant again.

The shift in moth numbers was carefully documented through catching them in traps. Release-recapture experiments confirmed that in polluted forests, more of the dark form survived for recapture, and *vice versa*. In addition, birds were filmed preferentially eating the less camouflaged moths off tree trunks.[9]

The story has generated boundless evolutionary enthusiasm. H.B. Kettlewell, who performed most of the classic experiments, said that if Darwin had seen this, "He would have witnessed the consummation and confirmation of his life's work."[10]

---

9. Reproduced by permission. C. Wieland, "Goodbye, Peppered Moths," *Creation* 21(3):56 (June–August 1999).
10. *Evolution and the Fossil Record, Readings from* Scientific American, "Darwin's Missing Evidence," H.B. Kettlewell (San Francisco, CA: W.H. Freeman and Co., 1978), p. 23.

Actually, even as it stands, the textbook story demonstrates nothing more than gene frequencies shifting back and forth, by natural selection, within one created kind. It offers nothing which, even given millions of years, could add the sort of complex design information needed for amoeba-to-man evolution.

Even L. Harrison Matthews, a biologist so distinguished he was asked to write the foreword for the 1971 edition of Darwin's *Origin of Species*, said therein that the peppered moth example showed natural selection, but *not* "evolution in action."

However, it turns out that this classic story is full of holes anyway. *Peppered moths don't even rest on tree trunks during the day.*

Kettlewell and others attracted the moths into traps in the forest either with light, or by releasing female pheromones — in each case, they only flew in *at night*. So where do they spend the day? British scientist Cyril Clarke, who investigated the peppered moth extensively, wrote:

> But the problem is that we do not know the resting sites of the moth during the day time. . . . In 25 years we have found only two *betularia* on the tree trunks or walls adjacent to our traps (one on an appropriate background and one not), and none elsewhere.[11]

The moths filmed being eaten by the birds were laboratory-bred ones placed onto tree trunks by Kettlewell; they were so languid that he once had to warm them up on his car hood.[12]

11. C.A. Clarke, G.S. Mani, and G. Wynne, "Evolution in Reverse: Clean Air and the Peppered Moth," *Biological Journal of the Linnean Society* 26:189–199, 1985; quote on p. 197.
12. *Calgary Herald*, March 21, 1999, p. D3.

And all those still photos of moths on tree trunks? One paper described how it was done — *dead moths were glued to the tree.*[13] University of Massachusetts biologist Theodore Sargent helped glue moths onto trees for a NOVA documentary. He says textbooks and films have featured "a lot of fraudulent photographs."[14]

Other studies have shown a very poor correlation between the lichen covering and the respective moth populations. And when one group of researchers glued dead moths onto trunks in an unpolluted forest, the birds took more of the dark (less camouflaged) ones, as expected. But their traps captured *four times as many dark moths as light ones* — the opposite of textbook predictions![15]

The University of Chicago's Jerry Coyne said that such painful revelations about the moth story ("the prize horse in our stable") was like finding out that Santa Claus was not real. Quoted by creationists, he now insists the peppered moths do somehow demonstrate "evolution" after all.

Regrettably, hundreds of millions of students have once more been indoctrinated with a "proof" of evolution which is riddled with error, fraud and half-truths.[16]

REJECTED ARGUMENT 3: VESTIGIAL ORGANS

Evolutionists often argue that such things as flightless birds' small wings, pigs' toes, male nipples, legless

---

13. D.R. Lees and E.R. Creed, "Industrial Melanism in Biston Betularia: The Role of Selective Predation," *Journal of Animal Ecology* 44:67–83, 1975.
14. J.A. Coyne, *Nature,* 396(6706):35–36; *The Washington Times,* January 17, 1999, p. D8.
15. Lees and Creed, reference 13.
16. Unfettered by evolutionary "just so" stories, researchers can now look for the real causes of these population shifts. Might the dark form actually have a function, like absorbing more warmth? Could it reflect conditions in the caterpillar stage? In a different nocturnal moth species, Sargent has found that the plants eaten by the larvae may induce or repress the expression of such "melanism' in adult moths (see T.R. Sargent et al. in M.K. Hecht et al., *Evolutionary Biology* (New York, NY: Plenum Press, 1998).

lizards, the rabbit's digestive system, the human appendix, and hip bones and teeth in whales are useless and have no function. They claim these features are "leftovers of evolution" and evidence for evolution.

The "vestigial" organ argument[17] for evolution is an old chestnut, but it is not valid.

First, it is impossible to prove that an organ is useless. The function may simply be unknown and its use may be discovered in the future. This has happened with more than 100 formerly alleged useless vestigial organs in humans, that are now known to be essential.

Second, even if the alleged vestigial organ were no longer needed, it would prove "devolution" not evolution. The creation model allows for deterioration of a perfect creation since the Fall. However, the particles-to-people evolution model needs to find examples of *nascent* organs, i.e., those which are *increasing* in complexity.

Wings on birds that do not fly?

There are at least two possibilities as to why flightless birds such as ostriches and emus have wings:

1. The wings are indeed "useless" and derived from birds that once could fly. This is possible in the creationist model. Loss of features is relatively easy by natural processes, whereas acquisition of new characters, requiring specific new DNA information, is impossible. Loss of wings most probably occurred in a beetle species that colonized a windy island. Again, this is *loss* of genetic information, so it is not evidence for microbe-to-man evolution, which requires masses of new genetic information.[18]

---

17. Adapted with permission from chapter 7 of Ken Ham, Andrew Snelling, and Carl Wieland, *The Answers Book* (Green Forest, AR: Master Books, 1990).
18. C. Wieland, "Beetle Bloopers: Even a Defect Can Be an Advantage Sometimes," *Creation* 19(3):30, 1997.

2. The wings have a function. Some possible functions, depending on the species of flightless bird, are: balance while running, cooling in hot weather, warmth in cold weather, protection of the rib cage in falls, mating rituals, scaring predators (emus will run at perceived enemies of their chicks, mouth open and wings flapping), sheltering of chicks, etc. If the wings are useless, why are the muscles functional, allowing these birds to move their wings?

Pigs with two toes that do not reach the ground?

Does this mean that the shorter toes have no function? Not at all. Pigs spend a lot of time in water and muddy conditions for cooling purposes. The extra toes probably make it easier to walk in mud (a bit like the rider wheels on some long trucks that only touch the road when the truck is heavily loaded). Perhaps the muscles attached to the extra toes give strength to the "ankle" of the pig.

Why do males have nipples?

Males have nipples because of the common plan followed during early embryo development. Embryos start out producing features common to male and female — again an example of "design economy." Nipples are a part of this design economy. However, as Bergman and Howe point out, the claim that they are useless is debatable.[19]

What is the evolutionist's explanation for male nipples? Did males evolve (devolve) from females? Or did ancestral males suckle the young? No evolutionist would propose this. Male nipples are neither evidence for evolution nor evidence against creation.

19.J. Bergman and G. Howe, " 'Vestigial Organs' are Fully Functional," Creation Research Society Monograph No. 4 (Terre Haute, IN: Creation Research Society Books, 1990).

Why do rabbits have digestive systems that function "so poorly that they must eat their own feces"?

This is an incredible proposition. One of the most successful species on earth would have to be the rabbit! The rabbit's mode of existence is obviously very efficient (what about the saying "to breed like rabbits"?) Just because eating feces may be abhorrent to humans, it does not mean it is inefficient for the rabbit! Rabbits have a special pouch called the *caecum*, containing bacteria, at the beginning of the large intestine. These bacteria aid digestion, just as bacteria in the rumen of cattle and sheep aid digestion. Indeed, rabbits "chew the cud" in a manner that parallels sheep and cattle.

The rabbit produces two types of fecal pellet — a hard one and a special soft one coming from the caecum. It is only the latter that is eaten to enrich the diet with the nutrients produced by the bacteria in the caecum. In other words, this ability of rabbits is a design feature; it is not something they have learned to do because they have "digestive systems that function so poorly." It is part of the variety of design, which speaks of creation, not evolution.

Skeptics have claimed the Bible is in error in saying that the rabbit "chews the cud" (Lev. 11:6). The Hebrew literally reads, "raises up what has been swallowed." The rabbit *does* re-eat what has been swallowed — its partly digested fecal pellets. The skeptics are wrong again.

Legless lizards

It is quite likely that legless lizards could have arisen through loss of genetic information from an original created kind, and the structures are consistent with this. "Loss" of a structure is of no comfort to evolutionists, as they have to find a mechanism for creating new structures, not losing them. Loss of information cannot explain how evolution "from ameba to man" could occur. Genesis 3:14 suggests that snakes may have once had legs.[20]

Adaptation and natural selection are biological facts; amoeba-to-man evolution is not. Natural selection can only work on the genetic information present in a population of organisms — it cannot create new information. For example, since no known reptiles have genes for feathers, no amount of selection will produce a feathered reptile. Mutations in genes can only modify or eliminate existing structures, not create new ones. If in a certain environment a lizard survives better with smaller legs, or no legs, then varieties with this trait will be selected for. This might more accurately be called *devolution,* not *evolution.*

Rapid minor changes in limb length can occur in lizards, as demonstrated on Bahamian islands by Losos and others.[21] The changes occurred much faster than evolutionists thought they could. Such changes do not involve new genetic information and so give no support to microbe-to-man evolution. They do illustrate how quickly animals could have adapted to different environments after the Flood.

The human appendix

It is now known that the human appendix contains lymphatic tissue and helps control bacteria entering the intestines. It functions in a similar way to the tonsils at the upper end of the alimentary canal, which are known

20. C. Brown, "The origin of the snake" (letter), *Creation Research Society Quarterly* 26:54, 1989. Brown suggests that monitor lizards may have been the precursors of snakes.
21. J.B. Losos, K.I. Warheit, and T.W. Schoener, "Adaptive Differentiation Following Experimental Island Colonization in Anolis Lizards," *Nature* 387:70–73, 1997. See comment by T.J. Case, *Nature* 387:15–16, and *Creation* 19(4):9.

to fight throat infections. Tonsils also were once thought to be useless organs.[22]

Hip bones in whales

Some evolutionists claim that these bones show that whales evolved from land animals. However, Bergman and Howe point out that they are different in male and female whales. They are not useless at all, but help with reproduction (copulation).[23]

Teeth in embryonic baleen whales

Evolutionists claim that these teeth show that baleen whales evolved from toothed whales. However, they have not provided an adequate mechanism for scrapping one perfectly good system (teeth) and replacing it with a very different system (baleen or whalebone). Also, the teeth in the embryo function as guides for the correct formation of the massive jaws.

As Scadding, an evolutionist, said, ". . . vestigial organs provide no evidence for evolutionary theory."[24]

APPENDIX 2: COMMON ARGUMENTS FOR CREATION THAT SHOULD NOT BE USED

ARGUMENTS CREATIONISTS SHOULDN'T USE

There are many strong arguments for creation, but some are not so strong, and others are totally unsound.[25] It's important to know the difference. This is why it's important to keep up with current creationist literature.

---

22. K. Ham and C. Wieland, "Your Appendix . . . It's There for a Reason," *Creation* 20 (1):41–43, 1997; J.W. Glover, "The Human Vermiform Appendix — a General Surgeon's Reflections," *TJ* 3:31–38, 1988.
23. See C. Wieland, "The Strange Tale of the Leg on a Whale," *Creation* 20(3):10–13, 1998.
24. S.R. Scadding, "Do Vestigial Organs Provide Evidence for Evolution?" *Evolutionary Theory* 5:173–176, 1981.
25. Based on J. Sarfati, "Moving Forward: Arguments We Think Creationists Shouldn't Use," *Creation* 24(2):20–34 (March–May 2002).

There is so much good evidence for creation that there is no need to use any of the "doubtful" arguments.

Using discredited arguments rebounds on the user, and it's a poor testimony for the cause of Christ. It's the *truth* that sets us free (John 8:32), not error — and Christ is "the truth" (John 14:6)!

Christians should not become alarmed when they find out creationist researchers have overturned their favorite arguments. Rather, they should refocus on the main issue, the authority of the Word of God, the 66 books of the Bible,[26] not the theories of fallible humans, whether creationist or evolutionist.

OUR STARTING POINT

The authority of the Bible is the main emphasis of Answers in Genesis. We don't try to "prove" the Bible with science; rather, we accept the Bible's propositions as true without proof, i.e., as *axioms* or *presuppositions*.

All philosophical systems, not just Christianity, start with *axioms*. There are good reasons for accepting the axioms of Scripture as true, because it can be shown that they lead to a consistent view of physical and moral reality, which other axioms can't provide.

Genesis contains a number of Hebrew grammatical features that show it was intended to teach a straightforward history of the world from its creation. Genesis, backed up by the rest of Scripture, unambiguously teaches[27] that:

The heavens, earth, and everything in them were created in six consecutive normal days, the same as those of our work week (Exod. 20:8–11).

---

26. For a defense of the authority, inerrancy, and sufficiency of the Bible, and the correctness of the 66-book Canon, see the web address: <www.AnswersInGenesis.org/Bible>.

27. Justification for these can be found in the Q&A page on Genesis, AiG Web site, or our Creation CD. Both contain many past *Creation* magazine articles.

Earth is about 6,000 years old, since Jesus said mankind was there from the "beginning of creation," not billions of years later (Mark 10:6).

Adam sinned and brought physical death to mankind (Rom. 5:12–19; 1 Cor. 15:21–22).

Since man was the federal head of creation, the whole creation was cursed (Rom. 8:20–22), which included death to animals, with the end of the original vegetarian diet for both humans and animals (Gen. 1:29–30).

God judged the world by a globe-covering flood, which Jesus and Peter compared with the coming Judgment (Luke 17:26–27; 2 Peter 3:3–7). This destroyed all land vertebrate animals and people not on the ocean-liner–sized ark.

God then judged the people by confusing their language at Babel — after they had refused to spread out and repopulate the earth after the Flood.

USING THIS FRAMEWORK

It's important to realize that all "facts" of science do *not* speak for themselves, but are *interpreted* within a framework. Evolutionists start with the axiom of *naturalism* or *materialism*, i.e., God (if He even exists) performed no miraculous acts of creation.

Biblical creationists interpret the *same* facts and observations, but within the framework outlined above.

WHAT SHOULD WE DEFEND, AND WHAT SHOULD WE HOLD LOOSELY?

It's very important to distinguish the biblical framework from various creationist scientific models within this framework. To Christians, the *framework* should be non-negotiable, but the *models* should never be held dogmatically.

All theories of science are fallible, and new data often overturn previously held theories. Evolutionists continually revise their theories because of new data, so it should not be surprising or distressing that some creationist scientific theories need to be revised, too.

AiG has never promoted many of the fallacious creationist arguments listed here. Indeed, some have not been promoted by *any* major creationist organization; rather, they are straw men set up by anti-creationists.[28]

Ironically, some skeptics criticize creationists when they retract doubtful arguments, but the same people accuse creationists of being unwilling to change their minds.

SOME ARGUMENTS CREATIONISTS SHOULD AVOID[29]

"Darwin recanted on his deathbed."

Many people use this story, originally from Lady Hope. However, it is almost certainly not true, and there is no corroboration from those who were closest to him, even from Darwin's wife Emma, who never liked the evolutionary theory. Also, even if true, so what? If Ken Ham recanted creation, would that disprove it? So there is no value to this argument whatever.[30]

"Moon dust thickness proves a young moon."

For a long time, creationists claimed that the dust layer on the moon was too thin if dust had truly been falling on it for billions of years.

---

28. Those (such as Hugh Ross) who believe that God created over billions of years and thus have animal death occurring before sin, are also guilty of setting up straw men. See K. Ham, "Demolishing 'Straw Men,'" *Creation* 19(4):13–15, 1997.
29. For a fuller, frequently updated list, see <www.AnswersInGenesis.org/dont_use>.
30. R. Grigg, "Did Darwin Recant?" *Creation* 18(1):36–37, 1995.

The real "Lady Hope" of the "Darwin recanted" legend was buried in this grave located at the Rookwood Cemetery in Sydney, Australia.

They based this claim on early estimates — by evolutionists — of the influx of moon dust, and worries that the moon landers would sink into this dust layer.

But these early estimates were wrong, and by the time of the Apollo landings, most in NASA were not worried about sinking. So the dust layer thickness can't be used as proof of a young moon (or of an old one either).[31]

"The Japanese trawler *Zuiyo-maru* caught a dead plesiosaur near New Zealand in 1977."

This carcass was almost certainly a rotting basking shark, since their gills and jaws rot rapidly and fall off, leaving the typical small "neck" with the head (see photo, right).

This has been shown by similar specimens washed up on beaches. The effect is so well-known that these carcasses have been called "pseudoplesiosaurs."

Also, detailed anatomical and biochemical studies of the *Zuiyo-maru* carcass confirm that it could not have been a plesiosaur.[32]

A decomposed basking shark, rotting to give a "plesiosaur look."
(Photo by Bev Elliott)

31. "Moon Dust Argument No Longer Useful," *Creation* 15(4):22, 1993; A. Snelling and D. Rush, "Moon Dust and the Age of the Solar System," *TJ* 7(1):2–42, 1993.
32. P. Jerlström, "Live Plesiosaurs: Weighing the Evidence," *TJ* 12(3):339–346, 1998; P. Jerlström and B. Elliott, "Letting Rotting Sharks Lie: Further Evidence That the Zuiyo-maru Carcass Was a Basking Shark, Not a Plesiosaur, *TJ* 13(2): 83–87, 1999.

"Women have one more rib than men."

AiG has long pointed out the fallacy of this statement. Dishonest skeptics wanting to caricature creation also use it, in reverse. The removal of a rib would not affect the *genetic instructions* passed on to the offspring, any more than a man who loses a finger will have sons with nine fingers.

Note also that Adam wouldn't have had a permanent defect, because the rib is the one bone that can regrow if the surrounding membrane (periosteum) is left intact.[33]

"Woolly mammoths were snap-frozen during the Flood catastrophe."

This is contradicted by their geological setting. It's most likely that they perished toward the end of the Ice Age, possibly in catastrophic dust storms.[34] Partially digested stomach contents are not proof of a snap freeze, because the elephant's stomach functions as a holding area — a mastodon with preserved stomach contents was found in the midwestern United States, where the ground was not frozen.

"The 2nd law of thermodynamics began at the Fall."

This law says that the entropy ("disorder") of the universe increases over time, and some have thought that this was the result of the Curse. However, disorder isn't always harmful. An obvious example is *digestion*, breaking down large complex food molecules into their simple building blocks. Another is *friction*, which turns ordered mechanical energy into disordered heat — otherwise

33. C. Wieland, "Regenerating Ribs: Adam and That 'Missing' Rib," *Creation* 21(4):46–47, 1999.
34. M. Oard, "The Extinction of the Woolly Mammoth: Was It a Quick Freeze?" *TJ* 14(3):24–34, 2000.

Adam and Eve would have slipped as they walked with God in Eden! A less obvious example to laymen might be the sun heating the earth, but to a physical chemist, heat transfer from a hot object to a cold one is *the* classic case of the second law in action. Also, breathing is based on another classic second law process, gas moving from a high pressure to low pressure. Finally, *all* beneficial processes in the world, including the development from embryo to adult, increase the *overall* disorder of the universe because the disorder of the surroundings is increased more than that of the system is reduced, showing that the second law is not inherently a curse.

Death and suffering of *nephesh* animals before sin *would* be contrary to the biblical framework above. It is more likely that God withdrew some of His sustaining power (Col. 1:15–17) at the Fall so that the *net* effects of the second law would now lead to overall decay.

"Archaeopteryx was a fraud."

Some have claimed that feathers were attached to a dinosaur skeleton. However, the skeleton has a proper bird skull, perching claws, tiny bumps on the bones where the feathers were attached to the bones by ligaments, and evidence of pneumatized bones indicating the unique avian lung system. Also, patterns on the limestone slabs, including some on top of the feather imprints, match perfectly so must have formed on the bedding plane before the slab was split.[35]

It has been suggested that the fossil, which allegedly shows both bird-like and reptilian features, had its fine feather impressions added by a forger, making it one of the world's first paleontological hoaxes. The fossil specimens

---

35. See documentation in J. Sarfati, *Archaeopteryx* (unlike *Archaeoraptor*) is NOT a hoax — it is a true bird, not a "missing link," <www.answersingenesis.org/not_hoax>.

are, however, genuine — unlike the more recent and proven fraud, *Archaeoraptor*, featured in a leading world journal, where portions of different fossils were glued together to make a "bird-dinosaur missing link."

"Dubois renounced Java man as a "missing link" and claimed it was just a giant gibbon."

Evolutionary anthropology textbooks claimed this, and creationists followed suit. However, those who said this actually misunderstood Dubois, as Stephen Jay Gould showed. It's true that Dubois claimed that Java man (which he called *Pithecanthropus erectus*) had the proportions of a gibbon. But this was because he had an eccentric view of evolution, universally discounted today. His idea demanded that, in the alleged transitional sequence leading to man, the brain-size/body weight ratio would fit into a mathematical series. His "gibbon" claim was in order to make the Java man find fit this view, so as to *reinforce* its "missing link" status.[36]

"The phrase 'science falsely so called' in 1 Timothy 6:20 (KJV) refers to evolution."

To develop a scriptural model properly, we must understand what the author *meant* to communicate to his intended audience, which in turn is determined by the grammar and historical context. We must not try to read into Scripture that which appears to support a particular viewpoint. In this passage, the original Greek word translated "science" is *gnosis*, and *in this context* refers to the lite esoteric "knowledge" that was the key to the mystery religions, which later developed into the heresy of *Gnosticism*. This was not an *error* by the KJV translators, but one example of how words *change their meanings over time*. The word "science" *originally* meant

---

36. "Who Was 'Java man'?" *Creation* 13(3):22–23, 1991.

"knowledge," from the Latin *scientia*, from *scio* meaning "know." This is *not* the way it is used today, so modern translations *correctly* render the word as "knowledge" in this passage.

Of course AiG believes that evolution *is* anti-knowledge because it clouds the minds of many to the abundant evidence of God's action in creation and the true knowledge available in His Word, the Bible. But it still is wrong to use fallacious arguments to support a true viewpoint. On a related matter, it is linguistically fallacious to claim that, even now, "science *really* means knowledge," because meaning is determined by *usage*, not *derivation* (etymology).

"If we evolved from apes, why are there still apes today?"

Some evolutionists also miss the main point, by protesting that they don't believe that we descended from apes, but that apes and humans share a common ancestor. The evolutionary paleontologist G.G. Simpson had no time for this "pussyfooting," as he called it. He said, "In fact, that earlier ancestor would certainly be called an ape or monkey in popular speech by anyone who saw it. Since the terms ape and monkey are defined by popular usage, man's ancestors were apes or monkeys (or successively both). It is pusillanimous [mean-spirited] if not dishonest for an informed investigator to say otherwise."[37]

Many evolutionists believe that a small group of creatures split off from the main group and they became

37. W.R. Bird, *The Origin of Species: Revisited*, Vol. 1:233 (Nashville, TN: Thomas Nelson, 1991), citing G.G. Simpson, "The World into Which Darwin Led Us," *Science* 131:966–969.

reproductively isolated from the main large population. Most change supposedly happened in such a small group, which can lead to *allopatric speciation* (a geographically isolated population forming a new species). So nothing in evolutionary theory requires the main group to become extinct.

It is important to be aware that this mechanism is not the sole property of evolutionists — creationists believe that most human variation occurred after small groups became isolated (but not speciated) at Babel, while Adam and Eve probably had mid-brown skin color. The quoted erroneous statement is analogous to saying, "If all people groups came from Adam and Eve, then why are mid-brown people still alive today?"

So what's the difference between the creationist explanation of people *groups* (races) and the evolutionist explanation of people *origins*? Answer: the former involves separation of already-existing information and loss of information through mutations; the latter requires the generation of tens of millions of "letters" of *new* information.

"NASA computers, in calculating the positions of planets, found a missing day and 40 minutes, proving Joshua's 'long day' of Joshua 10 and Hezekiah's sundial movement of 2 Kings 20."

This is a hoax. Essentially the same story, now widely circulated on the Internet, appeared in the somewhat unreliable 1936 book *The Harmony of Science and Scripture* by Harry Rimmer. Evidently an unknown person embellished it with modern organization names and modern calculating devices.

Also, the whole story is mathematically impossible — it requires a *fixed reference point* before Joshua's long day. In fact we would need to cross-check between *both* astronomical *and* historical records to detect any missing day.

And to detect a missing 40 minutes requires that these reference points be known to within an accuracy of a few minutes. It is certainly true that the timing of solar eclipses observable from a certain location can be known precisely. But the ancient records did not record time that precisely, so the required cross-check is simply not possible. Anyway, the earliest historically recorded eclipse occurred in 1217 B.C., nearly two centuries after Joshua. So there is no way the missing day could be detected by any computer.

Note that discrediting this myth doesn't mean that the events of Joshua 10 didn't happen. Features in the account support its reliability, e.g., the moon was also slowed down. This was not necessary to prolong the day, but this would be observed from earth's reference frame if God had accomplished this miracle by slowing earth's rotation.[38]

"Paluxy tracks prove that humans and dinosaurs co-existed."

Some prominent creationist promoters of these tracks have long since withdrawn their support. Some of the allegedly "human footprints beside tracks" may be artifacts of erosion of dinosaur tracks obscuring the claw marks. There is a need for properly documented research on the tracks before we would use them to argue the co-existence of humans and dinosaurs. (However, there is much evidence that dinosaurs and humans co-existed.)

SUMMARY

This appendix is meant to encourage trust in God's infallible Word, not man's fallible theories — even our own. Its purpose is also to help people avoid defending

---

38. R. Grigg, "Joshua's Long Day: Did It Really Happen — and How?" *Creation* 19(3):35–37, 1997.

the cause of the truth with faulty arguments, and instead focus on the many effective arguments for biblical creation and against evolution/billions of years. To keep yourself up-to-date with both types of argument, keep up with AiG periodicals (including *TJ*), and visit <www.AnswersInGenesis.org>.

WHAT ARGUMENTS ARE DOUBTFUL, HENCE INADVISABLE TO USE?

Canopy theory

This is not a direct teaching of Scripture, so there is no place for dogmatism. Also, no suitable model has been developed that holds sufficient water; but some creationists suggest a partial canopy may have been present.

"There was no rain before the Flood."

This is not a direct teaching of Scripture, so again there should be no dogmatism. Genesis 2:5–6 at face value teaches only that there was no rain at the time Adam was created. But it doesn't rule out rain at any later time before the Flood, as great pre-uniformitarian commentators such as John Calvin pointed out. A related fallacy is that the rainbow covenant of Genesis 9:12–17 proves that there were no rainbows before the Flood. As Calvin pointed out, God frequently invested existing things with new meanings, e.g., the bread and wine at the Lord's Supper.

"Natural selection as tautology"

Natural selection is in one sense a tautology (i.e., Who are the fittest? Those who survive/leave the most offspring. What creatures survive/leave the most offspring? The fittest). But a lot of this is semantic word play, and depends on how the matter is defined, and for what purpose the definition is raised. There are many areas of life in which circularity and truth go hand in hand. (E.g., What is electric charge? That quality of matter on which an electric field acts. What is an electric field? A region in space that exerts a force on electric charge. But no one would deny that the theory of electricity is thereby invalid and can't explain how motors work.) It is only that circularity cannot be used as independent proof of something.

To harp on the issue of tautology can become misleading, if the impression is given that something tautological therefore doesn't happen. Of course, the environment can "select," just as human breeders select. Of course, demonstrating this doesn't mean that fish could turn into philosophers by this means — the real issue is the nature of the variation, the information problem. Arguments about tautology distract attention from the real weakness of neo-Darwinism — the source of the new information required. Given an appropriate source of variation (for example, an abundance of created genetic information with the capacity for Mendelian recombination), replicating populations of organisms would be expected to be capable of some adaptation to a given environment, and this has been demonstrated amply in practice.

Natural selection is also a useful explanatory tool in creationist modelling of post-Flood radiation with speciation.

"The speed of light has decreased over time" (c decay).

Although most of the evolutionary counter-arguments have been proven to be fallacious, there are still a number of problems, many of which were raised by creationists, which we believe have not been satisfactorily

39. For analysis of Paul Davies' recent claims about the possibility of light slowing down, see C. Wieland, "Speed of Light Slowing Down After All? Famous Physicist Makes Headlines," <www.answersingenesis.org/cdk>, August 9, 2002.

answered.[39] AiG currently prefers Dr. Russell Humphreys' explanation for distant starlight,[40] although neither AiG nor Dr. Humphreys claims that his model is infallible.[41]

"There are no transitional forms"

Since there are *candidates*, even though they are highly dubious, it's better to avoid possible comebacks by saying instead: "While Darwin predicted that the fossil record would show numerous transitional fossils, even 140 years later, all we have are a handful of disputable examples."

"Gold chains have been found in coal."

Several artifacts, including gold objects, have been documented as having been found within coal, but in each case the coal is no longer associated with the artifact. The evidence is therefore strictly anecdotal (e.g., "This object was left behind in the fireplace after a lump of coal was burned"). This does not have the same evidential value as having a specimen with the coal and the artifact still associated.

"Plate tectonics is fallacious."

AiG believes that Dr. John Baumgardner's work on catastrophic plate tectonics provides a good explanation of continental shifts and the Flood. However, AiG recognizes that some reputable creationist scientists disagree with plate tectonics.

"Creationists believe in microevolution but not macroevolution."

These terms, which focus on "small" versus "large" changes, distract from the key issue of *information*. That is, particles-to-people evolution requires changes that

---

40. D.R. Humphreys, *Starlight and Time* (Green Forest, AR: Master Books, 1994).
41. Ken Ham, Andrew Snelling, and Carl Wieland, *The Answers Book* (Green Forest, AR: Master Books, 1990), see chapter 5.

increase genetic information, but all we observe is *sorting* and *loss* of information. We have yet to see even a "micro" increase in information, although such changes should be frequent if evolution were true. Conversely, we do observe quite "macro" changes that involve *no* new information, e.g., when a control gene is switched on or off.

"The gospel is in the stars."

This is an interesting idea, but quite speculative, and many biblical creationists doubt that it is taught in Scripture, so we do not recommend using it.

HERE'S THE GOOD NEWS

Answers in Genesis seeks to give glory and honor to God as Creator, and to affirm the truth of the biblical record of the real origin and history of the world and mankind.

Part of this real history is the bad news that the rebellion of the first man, Adam, against God's command brought death, suffering, and separation from God into this world. We see the results all around us. All of Adam's descendants are sinful from conception (Ps. 51:5) and have themselves entered into this rebellion (sin). They therefore cannot live with a holy God, but are condemned to separation from God. The Bible says that "all have sinned, and come short of the glory of God" (Rom. 3:23) and that all are therefore subject to "everlasting destruction from the presence of the Lord and from the glory of His power" (2 Thess. 1:9). But the good news is that God has done something about it.

> For God so loved the world, that He gave his only-begotten Son, that whoever believes in Him should not perish, but have everlasting life (John 3:16).

Jesus Christ the Creator, though totally sinless, suffered on behalf of mankind the penalty of mankind's sin, which is death and separation from God. He did this to satisfy the righteous demands of the holiness and justice of God, His Father. Jesus was the perfect sacrifice; He died on a cross, but on the third day, He rose again, conquering death, so that all who truly believe in Him, repent of their sin and trust in Him (rather than their own merit), are able to come back to God and live for eternity with their Creator.

Therefore:

> He who believes on Him is not condemned,
> but he who does not believe is condemned already,
> because he has not believed in the name of the
> only-begotten Son of God (John 3:18).

What a wonderful Savior — and what a wonderful salvation in Christ our Creator!

(If you want to know more of what the Bible says about how *you* can receive eternal life, please write or call the *Answers in Genesis* office nearest you — see page 239.)

INDEX

a priori, 54, 57, 83
abortion, 70
ad baculum (logical fallacy), 11
ad hominem (logical fallacy), 11
Adam, 21, 36–37, 42, 45–47, 89, 93, 147, 191, 212, 215–216, 219, 221, 225
adaptation, 75–76, 79, 209, 222
age of the earth/universe and starlight, 223
AIDS, 95–96
Ambulocetus, 135, 138–141
animal distribution, 21, 82
Antennapedia, 102
antibiotic resistance, 95–97, 102
"ape-men," 185–186, 188
appendix (human), 206, 209–210
Archaeopteryx, 130–134, 216
Archaeoraptor hoax, 216–217
ark, 17–18, 21, 79, 82, 99, 148, 212
asexual reproduction, 174
atheism, 23, 35, 195
Australopithecus ramidus, 188
axioms, 12, 57, 136, 148, 211
bacteria, 88, 92, 94–97, 99, 113, 115, 122, 124, 174–175, 208–209
bad things, 36–37, 44, 58, 93, 98, 147
bara, 44
Basilosaurus, 140–141
Baumgardner, John, 223
beetles, wingless, 91
Behe, Michael, 164, 167
bias, 28, 53–54, 57, 64, 136–137, 145
Bible history, 20–21
big bang, 14, 48, 185, 196
biogenetic law, 199–200
biological evolution, 195–197
blood clotting, evolution of, 168, 170–172

bonobos and chimps, 180–181
brain (human), 179, 192
Cambrian explosion, 143–144
carbon dating, 143, 146, 188
carnivory, 93
catastrophism, 27–28, 106, 145–147, 156, 215, 223
cave men, 191
chimps and bonobos, 180
cholera, 98–99
common structures/ancestry, 109–110
complexity, 6, 56, 66, 123–124, 157–159, 161–164, 166–167,
        169–172, 206
    definition, 32, 53, 60, 78, 84, 128, 157, 221
    irreducible, 6, 124, 161–162, 167, 169–170, 172
computer "simulations" of evolution, 156–157
continental drift, 79, 163
Creation magazine, 47, 87, 211
"creation science" (definition), 18–20, 63, 72, 78
crystals — see complexity
Curse, the, 89, 215–216
Damadian, Raymond, MRI pioneer, 26
Darwin, Charles, 17, 36, 69, 130
Dawkins, Richard, 9, 156, 178, 194
day (meaning in Genesis 1), 37
death, 21, 36–37, 45, 87, 91, 93, 96, 106, 110, 147–148, 176,
        212–213, 216, 225–226
deep time, 41, 152
Dennett, Daniel, 9, 36
Denton, Michael, 114
design, 5, 8, 20–22, 39, 56, 63, 70–71, 78, 89, 94, 106,
        109–110, 112, 117–122, 124–125, 132, 140, 142,
        160–162, 168–172, 180, 186, 202, 204, 207–208
dinosaurs
    extinction, 146
    fossils, 128
    Noah's ark, 148
    origin of birds theory, 66, 130
disease, germs — see pathogens

diversity, 72
DNA
    comparisons, 59, 107, 112
    human and chimp, 186
    hybridization, 78, 80, 180
    "junk," 117, 122–123
    mitochondrial, 110
ecosystems, 85, 98
education, creation/evolution, 8, 30–32, 46
elephant hurling, 69–70
embryo similarities and recapitulation, 199–203
equivocation, 12, 55, 95
evolution
    birds, 21, 65–66, 68, 75, 79, 129–132, 134, 142, 182,
        203–207
    definition and equivocation, 12, 55, 95
    human, 10, 20–21, 38, 56, 81, 90, 93, 110, 113–114, 119,
        127–129, 154, 165, 167, 172, 179, 181, 185–186,
        189–190, 192, 199, 201–202, 206, 209–210,
        219–220, 222
    mollusks, 113, 133
    relation to atheism, 9–10, 12, 19, 22–23, 25, 31, 33, 35,
        39, 49, 52, 54, 70, 89, 122, 156, 170, 178, 194–195
    whales, 129, 135–142, 206, 210
"Evolution" (PBS-TV)
    Episode 1, 36–38, 41, 95, 117, 138, 164, 185–186
    Episode 2, 41, 103, 142–143, 186
    Episode 3, 85–88, 144–145
    Episode 4, 89, 95, 97–99
    Episode 5, 173–178, 180
    Episode 6, 14, 185, 189–197
    Episode 7, 29–31, 44, 49
extinction, 14, 144–147, 215
    mass, 24, 38, 145, 147
    biblical explanation, 147–148
eye, 103–104, 117–121, 161–164, 166–167, 172
    complexity of, 163–164, 171
    alleged bad design, 121

"15 Answers to Creationist Nonsense," 7, 10–11, 13, 19, 51,
        59, 64, 69, 151
    Point 1, 51
    Point 2, 59
    Point 3, 59
    Point 4, 63
    Point 5, 65
    Point 6, 218
    Point 7, 151
    Point 8, 154
    Point 9, 158
    Point 10, 101
    Point 11, 81
    Point 12, 83
    Point 13, 130
    Point 14, 161
    Point 15, 167
fact (definition), 56–58
faith, 7, 9, 33, 35, 38–39, 43, 45, 47–49, 53, 62, 70, 78, 101,
        135, 172–173, 198
Fall, the, 39, 59, 71, 75, 79, 84, 90, 94, 98–99, 121, 206,
        214–216
feathered dinosaur, 131
Fitzroy, Captain Robert, 17–18, 39
flagellum, bacterial, 167–169
flightless birds, 132, 205–206
flood (Noah's), 27, 144, 146, 148
fossils
        human, 21, 127–129
        "living," 128, 148
        record, 21, 127–130, 148, 223
        transitional, 129–130, 132, 134–135, 144, 223
founder effect, 86
fraud, Haeckel, 200
Galapagos finches, 75, 80
gecko, 172
gene switches, 103

genes, 56, 79, 82, 89, 97, 99–100, 102–109, 113, 123–124,
        155, 167, 169, 173–177, 179, 181–183, 192,
        196–197, 209
Genesis 1, 18, 24, 37, 44, 49, 191
    days of creation week, 37, 93
    interpretation, 33, 41, 43, 54, 62, 112, 140, 199
genetic information, loss of, 45, 79, 99–100, 102, 155, 206,
        208
genetic mistakes, 103
geologic column, 128
"gill slits" in the human embryo, 199
global flood — see flood, Noah's
gospel, 14, 47, 70, 224
Gould, Stephen Jay, 9, 27–28, 32, 35, 38–41, 49, 54, 67–68,
        122, 130, 162, 217
GTE (general theory of evolution) — see evolution, definition
Haeckel, Ernst, 199–201
Ham, Ken, 8, 42–45, 47, 56, 60, 148, 179, 182, 210, 213
hemoglobin, evolution of, 108
heredity, 29, 109, 162
HIV resistance — see AIDS
homology, 112
        anatomical, 84, 109, 138, 161, 214
        molecular, 69, 94, 105, 107, 113–115, 138, 161, 168
hopeful monsters, 68
horse evolution, 132–133
hox gene, 102
human brain, 179, 192
human fossils, 21, 127–129
humanism, 31
humans and apes, 60, 109, 113, 183, 185, 187, 218
hybridization, 78, 80
Ice Age, 215
immune system, 94, 175
information theory, 56, 105
intelligent design, 8, 20–22, 63, 70–71, 78, 89, 122, 161, 168,
        170, 180
interpretation, 33, 41, 43, 54, 62, 112, 140, 199

irreducible complexity, 6, 124, 161–162, 167, 169, 172
Java man, 217
Jefferson High School, 31–32
Johnson, Philip E., 40, 71
Joshua's missing day, 219
judgment to come, 212
"junk" DNA — see DNA, "junk"
kinds, created — definition of, 21, 77, 79, 204, 208
language, 48, 154, 185, 190–195, 212
leafy spurge, 86–87
legless lizards, 208
Lewontin, Richard, 53–54, 57, 83
life, origin, 26, 58, 108, 151–152, 154–155, 157
living fossils, 148
locomotion, whale, 139, 142
logic, 11, 21–22, 33, 63–64
Lucy, 186–187
Lyell, Charles, 18, 27–28
macroevolution, 59, 105, 112, 223
male nipples, 205, 207
mankind, creation, 42, 46–47
marriage, 182
mass extinction, 147
Mayr, Ernst, 81, 84
meat eating, 93
mechanisms of evolution, 66, 82, 85, 155
memes, 196–197
microevolution — see macroevolution
migration, animal, 21, 82
Miller, Kenneth, 37–38, 40–41, 46, 95, 117–118, 120, 138–139, 169, 181–182
missing link, 134, 136, 138–139, 186–188, 216–217
mitochondria, 82–83
model, 29, 31, 67, 75–77, 79, 81, 84, 89–90, 97, 99–101, 189, 206, 217, 221, 223
molecular clock, 113–115
mollusks, evolution, 113, 133
moon dust, 213–214

morality, 39, 70, 173, 181, 183
mosaics, 131, 188
mosquito, 79
motor, 121, 160, 167–168, 170, 172
mutations
        beneficial, 5, 82, 92, 94, 98, 101, 147, 156, 163, 174, 216
naturalism, 11, 18–19, 23, 53, 212
natural law, 24
natural selection, 5, 45, 59, 69, 75–76, 79–83, 85, 88, 90,
        97–98, 101, 103, 106–108, 112, 117, 123, 155, 157,
        163, 171, 176, 179, 181, 191, 195, 204, 209, 221–222
Neandertal man, 189–192
nephesh, 94, 216
newt, 90–92, 94
Newton, Isaac, 25–26, 36, 52
Noah's ark, 18, 148
NOMA (non-overlapping magisterial), 38–40
order, origin of — see complexity
Origin of Species, 130, 162, 204, 218
"out of Africa" model, 189–190
Pakicetus, 136–137
Paluxy tracks, 220
panda's thumb, 122
paradigms and bias, 28, 53–54, 57, 64, 89, 128, 136–137,
        145, 168
Pasteur, Louis, 26
pathogens, 94, 98
PBS, see also *Evolution* (PBS-TV)
peppered moths, 203–204
philosophy and science, 53, 55, 198
"plesiosaur" carcass, 214
plate tectonics, 223
poison newt, 90
polyploidy, 104–105
Porter, Rufus, founder of *Scientific American,* 12, 71
predator-prey, 89–90, 96, 147, 166
presuppositions and science; see axioms
probability of evolution, 6, 151

progressive creation, 37
propaganda, evolutionary, 8, 72, 83
punctuated equilibrium, 67–68
rabbits, digestive system, 206, 208
races, origin; racism, 14, 69, 87–89, 175
rapid speciation, 76, 79
random order, 157
Refuting Evolution, 13, 70, 142
Rennie, John, 10–12, 14, 18–19, 22, 27, 60, 62, 69, 71–72, 158
rib, Adam's, 47, 215
Rodhocetus, 135, 141
saltationism, 66
Sarfati, Jonathan, 18, 21, 25, 38, 48, 64, 96, 102, 133, 148,
        152–153, 160, 162, 172, 187, 210, 216
science
        operation science (definition), 24
        origins science (definition), 12, 23, 25, 52
Scientific American, 7, 10, 12–14, 20–27, 51–53, 56, 59–68,
        70–72, 76, 80–84, 101, 105, 107–108, 112–113,
        127–130, 132–135, 151, 154, 156–158, 161–163,
        167, 169–170, 187, 194, 199, 203
        see also "15 Answers to Creationist Nonsense"
scientific evidence for creation, 7–8, 22, 45–46, 54–55, 57–64,
        66, 69
Scopes trial, 29–30
Scott, Eugenie, 9, 31, 35, 55, 60, 111, 169, 197
seven-day week, 172, 211
sex
        asexual reproduction, 174
        behavior, 181
        morality, 173
        sexual reproduction, 173–176
sickle-cell anemia, 91
simulations of evolution, 156–157
sin, 37, 45, 89, 93, 147, 213, 216, 225–226
"six days," 172, 211
speciation, 5, 21, 59, 65, 75–77, 79, 82–84, 88, 219, 222
species (definition), 60, 84

Spetner, Lee, 105–106, 180
spontaneous generation, 26, 61–62
Sputnik, 29–30
straw-man arguments, 11, 18, 27, 81, 83, 101
survival, struggle for, 36
symbiosis, 80, 88
tautology, 59, 221–222
tetrapod, evolution of, 142
theistic evolution, 36
theory (definition), 5, 9, 15, 20, 22, 25–26, 51–52, 55–59, 63, 66–69, 71, 76, 79, 82, 85, 89, 101, 105, 107, 114–115, 125, 130, 143, 146, 166, 179–180, 210, 213, 219, 221–222
thermodynamics, second law of, 157–159, 216
TJ (formerly Creation Ex Nihilo Technical Journal), 10, 14, 21, 25, 38, 64, 67, 94, 99, 108, 120, 122–123, 129, 135, 139, 142, 146, 152–153, 157, 160, 163, 166, 187, 189, 196, 210, 214–215, 221
transitional forms, 46, 57, 60, 66, 127, 129–130, 134, 136, 143–145, 163, 176, 223
tuberculosis, 96
two model approach, 22
uniformitarianism, 27
vapor canopy theory, 221
variation, 45, 76, 78, 82, 98, 133, 176, 219, 222
vestigial organs, 117, 122, 205–207, 210
viruses, 99
week, seven-day, 172, 211
whale, evolution, 135–136, 142
Wheaton College, 45–46
wingless beetles, 91
wingless birds, 131, 205–207
woolly mammoths, 215
world view, Christian v. secular, 8, 10, 12, 19–20, 27, 33, 39–40, 49, 53–54, 57, 60, 62, 66, 70, 128, 138, 154, 195, 212

WALKING
THROUGH SHADOWS
FINDING HOPE IN A WORLD OF PAIN
BY KEN HAM AND CARL WIELAND

- *A vital message of hope for a chaotic world in despair*
- *Read the dramatic testimony of Carl Wieland, who miraculously survived a head-on collision in the Australian outback.*
- *Discover God's grace in Robert Ham's story, as told by his brother Ken.*
- *Provides a biblical answer to the universal question of "Why do we suffer?"*

Since the terrorist attacks on the United States, more than ever people are asking basic, though deep, questions. Why would God allow this suffering? What does life on this planet mean?

Authors Ham and Wieland have both suffered through intense personal tragedy. Their peace and acceptance comes through in their approach to answering the difficult questions. By drawing on their own experiences, and those of others, then using the Bible to answer the hard questions and show why reality has been skewed by anti-God philosophies, they present remarkable answers for hurting people. An amazing read.

ISBN: 0-89051-381-3 • 144 pages • $11.99
casebound with jacket
Available at Christian bookstores nationwide

ABOUT THE AUTHOR

Born in Australia, Jonathan Sarfati moved to New Zealand as a child and later obtained his Ph.D. in physical chemistry at Victoria University in Wellington. In 1996, he returned to Australia and took a position as a research scientist and editorial consultant for the Creation Science Foundation in Brisbane. He now works full-time for Answers in Genesis, writing and reviewing articles for *Creation* magazine and the *TJ* technical journal. His first book, *Refuting Evolution*, has sold over 350,000 copies. He coauthored *The Answers Book*, and is a former New Zealand national chess champion.

ABOUT THE EDITOR

Mike Matthews is a writer and educator, with extensive experience in Christian publishing. His writings include several yearbooks on current events and a geography textbook used in Christian schools. He now serves as a writer/editor at Answers in Genesis, USA.

For a free catalog of material supporting biblical creation, or for more information about what the Bible teaches, contact one of the Answers in Genesis Ministries below. Answers in Genesis Ministries are evangelical, Christ-centered, non-denominational, and non-profit.

Creation Ministries International
4355 J Cobb Parkway
PMB 218
Atlanta, GA 30339-3887
1-800-6161-CMI (264)
www.CreationOnTheWeb.org

in Genesis
39005
Auckland
aland

Answers in Genesis
P.O. Box 6302
Acacia Ridge DC
QLD 4110
Australia

Answers in Genesis
5-420 Erb St. West
Suite 213
Waterloo, Ontario
Canada N2L 6K6

Answers in Geneis
P.O. Box 3349
Durbanville (Cape Town)
South Africa

Answers in Genesis
P.O. Box 5262
Leicester LE2 3XU
United Kingdom

website: <www.AnswersInGenesis.org>

In addition, you may contact:

Institute for Creation Research
P.O. Box 2667
El Cajon, CA 92021